HIGHER
ETIQUETTE

HIGHER ETIQUETTE

A Guide to the World of Cannabis,
from Dispensaries to Dinner Parties

LIZZIE POST

copresident of the Emily Post Institute

ILLUSTRATIONS BY SAM KALDA

TEN SPEED PRESS
California | New York

This book is dedicated to all the good people in the world who believe in consideration, respect, and honesty as life's guiding principles. The world is a better place because of you. (Whether you consume cannabis or not.)

THE WARNINGS

There may be risks associated with consuming cannabis. Smoke in particular can be hazardous to your health, and secondhand smoke can be harmful to those around you.

Effects may be felt anywhere from immediately to up to two or more hours after consumption. It is illegal to drive a motor vehicle or operate heavy machinery while under the influence of cannabis.

Children can be affected by cannabis differently from adults and it has the potential to make them very sick. Store cannabis products in a locked area where children cannot see or access them. If your child has consumed cannabis, call the Poison Control hotline at 1-800-222-1222. Symptoms may include having trouble walking or sitting up, becoming sleepy, or having a hard time breathing.

Cannabis may harm your baby if used in any form during pregnancy or while breastfeeding.

Cannabis can be harmful to animals. Pets that consume it can experience a range of effects, from lethargy to coma to death.

Consult your physician or licensed medical provider if choosing to use cannabis to treat a medical condition.

Synthetic cannabis, synthetic cannabinoids, or fake cannabis is not safe for human consumption.

All efforts have been made to ensure the accuracy of the information contained in this book as of the date of publication. The publisher and the author disclaim liability for any outcomes that may occur as a result of following the advice in this book.

CONTENTS

What would Emily Post think of this book?

Emily Post actively fought against the prohibition of alcohol during her time. While she abhorred smoke and would likely not have approved of burning cannabis, she grew up in an era when cannabis was often used for medicinal purposes in tincture form. I have found no evidence of her opinion on cannabis.

However, here are two passages from Emily's biography *Emily Post: Daughter of the Gilded Age, Mistress of American Manners*, by Laura Claridge, that illustrate Emily's perspective on Prohibition:

"Emily didn't drink, but, ever her father's daughter, she was disgusted with the government's interference with what she believed were citizens' rights."

"Finally here was an issue where she agreed with President Roosevelt: he should endorse the Twenty-First Amendment at once, stimulating the economy even as he rooted out the corruption bred in Prohibition's wake. As part of a coterie of prominent New York women convinced that for thirteen years the ill-conceived law had wreaked havoc on the nation, she urged that political candidates be judged primarily upon their position on repealing the Eighteenth Amendment."

Etiquette & Cannabis

When I began this project and started telling friends and family the subject matter, I received emphatic encouragement from many. For those who consume cannabis, weed etiquette is real, and it was high time someone wrote a book about it. Others had a harder time understanding the connection between pot and etiquette. To better bridge the gap, I'd like to introduce you to Emily Post etiquette and show you how it connects with the world of cannabis culture.

Emily Post said, "Whenever two people come together and their behavior affects one another, you have etiquette. It is not some rigid code of manners." It was this attitude that has made Emily Post North America's go-to source for etiquette advice for the past ninety-five years. With a hit 1930s radio program *The Right Thing to Do*, a bestselling book *Etiquette* (now in its nineteenth edition), and an ability to be both relatable and aspirational, Emily Post helped define American manners. Though Emily died in 1960, her practical and kind approach toward social graces has been carried on by her family through the Emily Post Institute. There, my cousin Daniel Post Senning and I are the fifth generation to run the company. Given Emily's definition, it's safe to say that cannabis culture is baked in etiquette, has been for a long time, and goes far beyond puff-puff-pass.

So what is etiquette? At the Emily Post Institute, we say that etiquette is made up of two things: manners and principles.

Manners are fascinating. They are the actions, words, and expectations that we create as a society for interacting with one another. Manners help us to know what is expected from us and what we can expect from others in a given situation. Manners can be good or bad. They are specific to periods of time, and they vary by country, by culture, and even by social group or family. When changes occur in a culture (like the legalization of cannabis), new manners emerge, and others become traditions of the past or obsolete.

Principles are reassuring. They are the concepts that can help guide us toward good interactions when there are no specific manners. The principles that we believe influence etiquette are *consideration, respect,* and *honesty*. When our intentions are based on these principles, even when things go badly, others can understand our good intent. These three principles can be applied to any situation in which you may find yourself. If you think about how the people in a given situation are affected (consideration), acknowledge the potential effects of possible solutions on those involved (respect), and choose to act in a way that genuinely benefits the most people in the situation (honesty), you're likely going to find a solution that will solve the problem at hand as well as honor and build the relationships involved.

In short: etiquette is about being aware of all the factors contributing to a situation and how the possible outcomes could impact each of the players. Good etiquette looks for the outcome that positively benefits the most people.

The Principles of Cannabis Etiquette

As an etiquette expert, I find that it can be easy to get trapped discussing negative behavior and how to fix it, especially when exploring new topics. Social media and tech (newer etiquette topics) can often feel that way. However, when exploring cannabis etiquette, *respect*, *generosity*, and *gratitude* were the three themes that came up most often, along with *sharing*. It was so encouraging to hear people excitedly talk about etiquette in a positive way. Rather than hearing complaints about rudeness and being offended, conversations focused on how to be aware and respectful of those around you. (So refreshing!)

RESPECT

Respect is deeply rooted in the cannabis community. There's respect for the plant itself, respect for individual consumption preferences, as well as respect for identity, style, and language choices. There is respect for the culture as it has been, as well as for where it's headed. In this community, we see and encourage respect for the *choice* to engage with cannabis whether you decide to or not. As the diverse cannabis community is being heard, we are increasingly aware that respect is a key component of the conversation around cannabis consumers and culture.

GENEROSITY

The generosity of the cannabis community comes from a collective understanding of how much cannabis helps people and how much it is enjoyed. Under cannabis prohibition, a consumer has to balance being generous with what little bud they have and need. More often than not, a person will choose to share the last of what they have—or at least share a hit or two—knowing what it can be like to go without. In a legalized culture with prevalent availability, this generosity doesn't disappear. Instead, it expands. Cannabis hosts are able to offer a greater array to their guests and still stay within their personal budgets. Friends smoke each other up freely, without expecting that the favor should be returned. (Though it almost always is.)

GRATITUDE

The cannabis community feels gratitude toward both the plant itself and the freedom to engage with it. From the language people use and the care taken with proposed legislation to the exploration of cannabis science and medicine, cannabis supporters are grateful for the opportunity to make the plant and its possibilities available in a way that makes sense for communities.

Despite legalization, consumers still respect the generosity of the community with displays of gratitude. Even if you have a ton of product at home, a friend's offer or gift of cannabis is often received with genuine appreciation. Even when the strain isn't one the receiver enjoys or can use, interviewees for this book still said they were always grateful for any cannabis that was offered to them. Of course, some of these people have likely declined certain strains at one point or another. But when asked from an etiquette standpoint about the right thing to do, most recommended accepting the gift and thanking the giver even if they didn't like it—the importance is placed on honoring the act of generosity.

SHARING

People love to share. When something is good in your life, you talk about it and invite others to experience it. Much like sharing food or drink, a scenic view, or a song, sharing cannabis is something enthusiasts are drawn to do.

You can certainly engage with cannabis privately, but the shared experience is encouraged and appreciated. It is the sharing of cannabis that makes it a topic ripe for etiquette to explore.

For the past century, cannabis has been shared and consumed in "secret." As legalization has taken place, cannabis lovers have been coming out of the canna-closet and sharing their methods, knowledge, and experiences. It's a true cannabis renaissance! As we discover ways to absorb cannabis into the greater folds of American life, collectively we will establish good etiquette and identify the beneficial manners that will shape this higher etiquette of cannabis culture.

THE CANNABIS CULTURE SHIFT

CHAPTER 1

It's a whole new world of weed.

Cannabis culture has existed since people first started sharing their uses for the plant. The more it was shared, the more common considerations were developed, observed, and passed on, friend to friend, community to community, all over the world. By the time I was born in 1982, cannabis may have been a subculture subject but its etiquette was widely known and communicated. Like all etiquette, it is culturally (even regionally and socially) specific and time sensitive, but one thing has remained constant: people aim to be polite about pot.

For the past century, cannabis etiquette has been largely based on its consumption during an era of prohibition. When cannabis is scarce and using it must remain secretive, much of the etiquette is focused on protecting people's privacy. Across the globe, cannabis has different levels of acceptance. In the United States, as individual states take the matter into their own hands, the accessibility of product, increased knowledge, and destigmatization are changing the culture of cannabis and its etiquette.

Etiquette Under Prohibition

Cannabis prohibition in the United States began in the early 1900s and has continued in many states (and federally) throughout the present day. Cannabis went from being a pharmacological recommendation and familiar health aid to being *marijuana, the dangerous drug.* There are many sources available to read up on the history of cannabis with the U.S. government and the American people. But from an etiquette standpoint, what matters is that its prohibition created an environment of secrecy and scarcity. The diverse language we have for cannabis and the generosity of spirit in the culture stem from the necessity to be discreet and from a lack of available legal product.

Once upon a time, having a joint passed to you by a stranger at a concert was like hitting the jackpot! Getting a new "weed guy" meant asking how he or she preferred to be reached and what degree of discretion should be used in conversations and transactions. Did you have to stay and hang out or was it a grab 'n' go situation? Maybe you were in a city where there was a delivery service. The reality of different tokes for different folks meant you always had to politely inquire about and keep track of your friends' and suppliers' styles and preferences.

Under prohibition, we often felt shame, encountered negative stereotypes, and were denied research opportunities. All of these were contributing factors to cannabis culture and to the shift we are seeing today.

SHAME

Cannabis shame was born out of prohibition, and it's one of the toughest hurdles for the community and others to clear. Many who grew up during prohibition were taught that cannabis was bad and would make you lazy and stupid. Maybe your parents had done it in the 1960s or 1970s, but that was then; it seemed that they (and the world) have gotten over the green. When all you've heard is that pot is bad or only for the young and dumb, it's hard to feel confident explaining why weed works for you. Even as prohibition is ending, many cannabis enthusiasts feel the need to use self-deprecating language about their cannabis consumption or identity. And many feel they have to justify their consumption for a *reasonable* reason—enjoyment not seeming to be enough.

STONER STEREOTYPES

Under prohibition, hippies, musicians, surfers, and teens dominated the images in mainstream media for what it looked like to be a pothead. The movie *Reefer Madness* was propaganda from Grandma's heyday, while Cheech and Chong, Jerry Garcia, Willie Nelson, Spicoli in *Fast Times at Ridgemont High,* Dave Chapelle, Snoop Dogg, and Cypress Hill carved out the cannabis caricatures of later generations.

The idea that people who like herb shouldn't be viewed as stoners or burnouts wasn't even really a thought. The general thinking was that those who continued usage after college "never grew up," or it was problematic that they "*STILL* smoked pot." With such negative stereotypes and impressions haunting cannabis culture for so long, it's no wonder that many cannabis consumers have preferred to keep their preference for pot under wraps.

LITTLE RESEARCH

In the United States, cannabis is considered a Schedule I drug at the federal level. This class of drugs is considered the most addictive and dangerous, and most cannabis users object to herb being classified this way. Federal laws restrict most research on Schedule I drugs, meaning there is a limited chance to scientifically explore the benefits or potential harms of cannabis. Many people who are anticannabis complain that the "evidence" that cannabis contains natural health benefits is simply anecdotal or based on "hippie facts." This research restriction has made it hard to combat such dismissals of cannabis with scientific facts. Given that 22 percent of American adults admit usage, it would seem more beneficial to our population as a whole to study cannabis more thoroughly.

A lack of research and understanding coupled with a history of the entertainment industry portraying cannabis as a silly, stupid, or dangerous substance creates confusion and stereotyping around the subject. With that, it makes sense that some folks are concerned about a substance that the masses have so far been largely in the dark about, issued programming labeling it as bad, and portrayed it in entertainment as a joke.

IT'S NOT ALL ROSES

It's important to be mindful that while this book explores and celebrates legalized cannabis, in most states there are many people who are incarcerated for engaging with cannabis. According to the Drug Policy Alliance, 2016 saw 653,249 arrests for marijuana law violations (89 percent of which were for possession only). There are also many people who have not had a positive experience with cannabis—some have had a negative physical reaction when trying cannabis themselves or have seen cannabis usage negatively impact their lives or the lives of loved ones. Even with unprecedented support for cannabis at this point in time, it's always appropriate to be mindful of those it has affected negatively and to be considerate, respectful, and honest about that.

Etiquette with Legalization

Legalization opens a broader world of cannabis to engage with—from the science, product availability, and personal connections to the wide world of cannabis entrepreneurship—and brings with it a wave of adventure, exploration, and opportunity. With the freedom to openly admit usage, families, businesses, and friendships can now reach new levels of honesty and understanding regarding cannabis. When it comes to our social interactions, the more we know, the easier it will be to find the good etiquette that will help us all (regardless of opinion) enjoy good relationships in legalized communities.

The amount of knowledge the average consumer can gain simply from having access to a dispensary experience is as exciting and liberating as it is likely to be overwhelming. (Cannabinoids and terpenes and potency, oh my!) When cannabis has been legalized in your hometown long enough that folks who don't partake don't mind being at a party where ganja is around, it's not uncommon for guests to hear, "Joints are in the jar, beer's in the cooler, help yourself. We just ask that you light up outside." Just like food, drinks, and entertainment at gatherings, cannabis becomes an offering that guests can choose to take part in or not.

One of the more interesting aspects of a comfortable legalized culture is that of prevalence and availability and what they do to consumption choices and habits. In Oregon, I watched as a friend tossed a half-smoked joint that had gone out into the garbage. "What are you doing?" I shrieked. "I'm so sorry," he said. "I just figured we'd roll another." I had to laugh. To him, throwing out a half-smoked joint that needed to be relit made sense. We could easily roll another, and it would taste better. Many folks who live legal liken offering saved bowls and roaches (the ends of blunts, spliffs, and joints) to offering someone half a can of beer, the rest of their cocktail, or their leftover food. "Thanks . . . but no thanks, we can pack fresh." People who save, reclaim, or smoke down to the bottom can be thought of as old-timers.

PERSPECTIVES CHANGE

The perspective of cannabis consumers living in legalized communities is amazingly different from those who still consume under prohibition. Whether you're traveling from a place where cannabis is illegal to a place where cannabis is fully legal or vice versa, there is care to be taken with assumptions, reactions, and interactions. Some folks who once may have been stoked to be passed a random joint at a concert now describe that same concert-passed joint with language they learned in the days of D.A.R.E. (Drug Abuse Resistance Education): "You don't know who it came from, what's really in it, if it's safe . . ." It's a cultural mental shift that encourages a more informed, more aware consumer. But you shouldn't come off as rude or belittling to those who operate with less freedom or who still share freely. It goes the other way, too. When you visit a legal state, don't assume it's a cannabis free-for-all.

As more people come out of the canna-closet, the perspective of what it means to engage with cannabis changes. No longer are the classic stereotypes of the teenage stoner, the rapper, or the hippie the only images confronting us. Your kid's teacher, your Pilates instructor, your favorite etiquette expert, your uncle the lawyer, your niece the magna cum laude student, even your favorite athlete might be the people who you discover are cannabis consumers. Those are very different people to imagine being "high." A legalized and more open cannabis culture makes it easier to recognize that cannabis consumption is unique and personal and doesn't mean that someone is inept or unable to excel (or even function) in life.

People talk about engaging with cannabis in many ways: as a creative aid, as a motivational aid, because they enjoy it, as a dietary supplement, as a form of therapy, and as a medicine. Respect for the individual experience is strong in legalized cannabis culture. You don't have to take on the same position as the person next to you. The cannabis community is divided in many ways, and as cannabis becomes destigmatized, we will start to see and hear the many faces, voices, and perspectives of the community.

DISCRETION IS STILL THE BETTER PART OF VALOR

Because cannabis use is a personal choice, discretion is still important even in a legalized society. Be loud, be proud, but also pay attention to and respect the wishes of others when it comes to exposure. Alcohol is deeply ingrained in our society, yet it's still not consumed by all, accepted by all, comfortable for all, or even safe for all. Holding off consuming in front of others until you know it's okay is the best practice. Choosing privacy or discretion is not the same as hiding in shame. Just because you are proud to legally toke up doesn't mean you want to or have to share that with everyone in your life. It's your choice with whom you talk about it and when.

One of the interesting things about legalization is that it doesn't equate to people smoking everywhere all the time. The trend toward vaping and portable vape options is in part due to the cannabis community's desire *not* to be "in your face." One or two hits of vape can go almost unnoticed, as opposed to taking a hit from a bong or passing a blunt. The options of today's legalized communities give consumers choice, and many are choosing methods and practices that help them respect others who are around.

WHAT IT MEANS TO BE HIGH

There are many ways to describe the experience of using cannabis. Why people choose to embrace or avoid the word *high* to describe having cannabis in their body is a personal choice, just as with how you would describe your dietary choices or your intimate relationships.

The term *high* has been negatively pigeonholed in association with drugs, referencing a high that won't let you function, doesn't last, and will haunt you, making you crave and obsess over it. It has also been a celebrated term: "I'm high on life" describes and associates being high with happiness and positivity—good things.

Most cannabis consumers feel high on life. For some, that means they are more connected to the world around them or are able to be present because pain or anxiety has been alleviated. For others, the euphoric and energetic possibilities from certain strains of cannabis boost their moods, stimulate creativity, and make them more positive influencers on the world around them. The highs that cannabis consumers talk about are not often foggy-headed, sleep-inducing hours of feeling checked out. (Though some strains at certain percentages can certainly make that happen.) The highs that cannabis consumers talk about are varied, in the same way that alcohol consumers don't equate one white wine spritzer with doing shots of tequila. Both are drinking, but they are very different experiences—especially depending on the quality of the product.

I hope that as more of our population take the time to consider their cannabis consumption, we are better able to articulate the effects cannabis has on us in ways that help us all understand the level of functionality that we have and how it impacts our social experiences.

No Matter What

Whether it is prohibited or legal, the spirit of cannabis culture remains true to the principles of respect, generosity, and gratitude. These have been at the heart of cannabis culture since cannabis was first shared, and they will always remain, as will the celebration and exploration of the plant that brings so much good to the lives of so many.

MEET CANNABIS

CHAPTER 2

Reader, I'd like to introduce Cannabis to you. Cannabis, this is Reader.

Like meeting your kid again all grown up after they've been away at school for years, cannabis is only just being seen by so many of us as more than a giggle-, munchie-, and sleep-inducing herb. As the scientific community researches the plant more and as we as a legalized culture interact with it more, the products, uses, and knowledge we gain grow and become better defined.

Get ready! This chapter is not what you might expect from your average etiquette book, but to really put this plant in the perspective of today's cannabis culture, it's important to cover the bases, and cannabis has a lot of bases. This chapter covers topics ranging from the lexicon of cannabis culture to the botany, chemistry, and human anatomy connected to cannabis and, of course, strains.

The Lingo . . . Canna-Lingo, That Is

There is an entire lexicon associated with cannabis culture, and there are differing views on what words and phrases are appropriate within the culture. An important thing to note: Never use a particular race, culture, nationality, socioeconomic status, or population to refer negatively to a type of cannabis, cannabis consumption, or consumer. It is not acceptable to degrade another person, population, or the cannabis plant in this way. Let's explore some new and classic cannabis lingo.

COMMON WORDS FOR CANNABIS

The language that developed during cannabis prohibition is fascinating and fun. Different regions and different social groups came up with their own vernacular regarding the big green plant. And that means there are a lot of different terms associated with cannabis and its consumption. Add to it the product boom of the past ten years, and that's a lot of lingo to absorb.

Cannabis The botanical name for the plant itself, *cannabis* is the most correct and respectful term for the plant. You are in good stead using this term with almost anyone. Some folks not yet hip to the legal scene might tease you a bit for being so formal, but for the most part, this is cannabis culture's go-to term when it comes to political correctness, polite conversation, and scientific accuracy.

Marijuana The etymology of this term is debated: the *Oxford English Dictionary* states that it may have come from the Nahuatl word *mallihuan*, which means prisoner, while author Weston La Barre claims it may have had its origins in the Chinese *ma ren hua*, meaning hemp seed flower. The term is used ubiquitously even in the news media and medical arenas, where typically writers prefer to use scientific terms. (Many choose it just because of its searchability ranking for marketing purposes.) The word *marijuana* is controversial within the cannabis community. Due to its history of being intentionally used to negatively associate cannabis with minorities and musicians, many find the term *marijuana* unacceptable and offensive. Others would like to see the term embraced in honor of the cultures that used the plant throughout history, where similar-sounding words to marijuana were used, or because they feel there is no longer a negative association with minorities and that the term has moved beyond that connection. Whether you'd like to eradicate it or see it reassociated, it's important to be aware that *marijuana* is not a scientific term and that it does have the potential to offend.

Weed Widely used and loved by many, the word *weed* is synonymous with cannabis, marijuana, and pot, but it's considered by some to be disrespectful to the plant itself. A weed is generally defined as any plant growing in a place you don't want it to or a plant of little or no value. This negative connotation isn't appreciated by some.

Pot This is a common word for cannabis. While its derivation is still debated, the *Oxford English Dictionary* says it comes from the Mexican-Spanish word *potiguaya*, meaning marijuana leaves. The word *pot* is not overly controversial and still gets used in media headlines from time to time; however, the term *pothead* can be insulting, depending with whom you are speaking.

Hemp A variety of the cannabis plant, humans have been cultivating hemp for thousands of years, primarily for its fibrous qualities. Hemp contains virtually no THC (tetrahydrocannabinol), the principal psychoactive constituent in cannabis. (See Cannabinoids on page 32.)

Hash A is a form of concentrated cannabis. It's made in various ways by collecting the trichomes—tiny plant glands containing THC that look like little crystals—and usually pressing them together. When hash is made just right, it's almost pure THC (if the strain was THC dominant), and it has intense flavor. Its varieties include: kief, bubble hash, finger hash, charas, and more.

More words for cannabis ganja, hashish, dope, dank, cheeba, sticky icky, bud, flower, nugget, nug, dubs, leaf, sweetleaf, green, greenleaf, Mary Jane, MJ, sensi, skunk, shake, tree, trees, broccoli, mota, herb, the herb, kind, kind bud, headies, outdoor, indoor, indo, devil's lettuce, chronic, chron, doja, and cheeba.

Words for crummy weed brick, bammer, crap weed, the brown, regs, regular, schwag, iawana, and shake.

SCIENTIFIC TERMS FOR CANNABIS

Here are some of the most common scientific terms you'll hear and read about regarding cannabis.

Cannabinoids These are natural chemical compounds found in cannabis. THC (tetrahydrocannabinol) and CBD (cannabidiol) are the two most researched and prominent cannabinoids found in the cannabis plant. There are 113 known cannabinoids.

Terpenes These organic aromatic chemical compounds are found in cannabis (and in all plants). There are more than 200 known terpenes associated with the cannabis plant.

Entourage Effect This is the combined effect of cannabis chemical compound combinations in humans. It is used to explain that the effects felt from an isolated compound (pure THC) are different from the effects felt if there are multiple cannabis chemical compounds (cannabinoids, terpenes, flavonoids, and others) all working together.

Decarboxylation This process of low-temperature heating changes the chemical compounds in the cannabis flower so that it is bioavailable. (If you ate straight bud, it wouldn't necessarily get you high, but if you ate decarboxylated bud, your body would feel the effects of the chemical compounds.) People who make edibles, tinctures, oils, and other products often "decarb" their flower first.

Activation Temperature This is the temperature to which a particular substance should be processed or consumed at in order to get the desired effect.

Combustion This is the process of burning something.

Vaporization This is the conversion of a solid or a liquid into a gas.

Cultivar This is a plant variety that has been produced in cultivation by selective breeding.

SELF-IDENTIFYING WORDS FOR CANNABIS USERS

To let others know that we are cannabis-friendly, the cannabis community uses a wide range of terms. The most respectful identifiers include cannabis enthusiast, cannabis activist, pro-cannabis, 420 friendly, fan of cannabis, cannabis consumer, and medicinal cannabis consumer or patient. Many commonly used terms for cannabis users can be offensive to some, including pothead, stoner, and burnout. Choose the words that work for you, but try to mirror the language others use for themselves when talking to or about them.

THE LEGEND OF 420

The origins of 420 begin with a group of friends, The Waldos, who met at 4:20 p.m. to search for a rumored abandoned cannabis crop. Unsuccessful in finding it, the group gave up but kept meeting at 4:20 p.m. to get high. Legend has it that Waldo member Dave Reddix was a roadie for Phil Lesh and is credited with associating 4:20 p.m. as the socially acceptable time to get high. It then spread through the Grateful Dead fanbase and now 420 is synonymous with cannabis. April 20 is known and widely celebrated as a cannabis holiday.

THE WORD HIGH

For those who don't consume, the word *high* can reflect being out of your mind or nonfunctioning. It registers anywhere from being potentially dangerous or reckless at worst to being mildly silly or uninhibited at best. For those who consume cannabis, getting high can mean anything from having a light buzz akin to feeling the effects of caffeine to being blazed beyond belief. It's important to remember, too, that not everyone feels strong psychoactive effects when they consume cannabis. CBD consumers rarely refer to using CBD as getting high. Given the broad range of effects that the natural chemical compounds found in cannabis can induce, it's hard to find one word to describe what people feel and experience.

People use the term *drinking* to describe many levels of alcohol consumption. "Jim's drinking" sounds like a problem, but if someone asks Beth Anne, "What are we drinking?" the question is about what Beth Anne is serving or Beth Anne's opinion on what the group should order. You'd never label someone who drinks two beers at a Friday night dinner party a drunk, and you wouldn't call someone who slams back twenty shots of tequila each weekend a person who is consuming responsibly. They are both drinking. They are both consuming alcohol but it's not the same thing.

You might know if someone consumes cannabis, but don't assume that you know *their* version of high.

The Botany of Cannabis

The cannabis plant comes from the larger Cannabaceae family, which includes almost 200 species of herbs, trees, shrubs, and flowering vines. This plant makes its presence known. From its sheer size (it can grow to over 10 feet tall) to the pungent and complex aromas that waft from its flowers, this is no shrinking violet. The plant's fibers, resins, and flowers can all be used, making the entire plant valued.

PISTILS

COLA

CALYX

SUGAR LEAVES

FAN LEAF

BLADES

TRICHOMES

STALK or STEM

THE ANATOMY OF THE CANNABIS PLANT

Here is the basic anatomy of the cannabis plant.

Flower Made up of colas (bud sites), which are made up of calyxes (which contain reproductive matter and are droplet shaped), and sugar leaves (small leaves coming out of the flowers). The flower is what most consumers are after, since it's the part of the plant that contains the most amount of trichomes (see below) and sugar leaves, which are coated in trichomes.

Pistils Also found on the flower, these are tiny orange, gold, or white hairs that collect pollen.

Fan leaf The symbol of the cannabis plant is the five-point fan leaf. It has five blades, and, depending on what subspecies it is, the formation of these blades will differ. (The largest of these are also called **water leaves**.)

Blade The single leaf that, combined with others, creates the fan-leaf formation.

Trichomes Plant glands that are found all over the plant; however, the ones we seek are from the flower and the inner leaves. Trichome glands primarily contain THC.

Stalk or stem The main stalk splits out into nodes that then allow for multiple colas to form. They contain no trichomes but can be used in hemp production.

SATIVA & INDICA CANNABIS PLANTS

There are two main types of cannabis plants, indica and sativa. These terms indicate the physical characteristics of the plant. The sativa plant is tall and lean, with thin stalks and thin, widespread fan leaves. The buds are often a light, bright green. The pistils—sometimes called hairs—are airy and long and are orange, gold, or white. *Cannabis sativa* loves warm, balmy climates (such as those of Thailand, Mexico,

Colombia, Peru, and certain regions in Africa) and is known for being hard to grow. In fact, much of the sativa cultivated for human consumption is hybridized with indica to make it easier to grow and able to grow bigger yields. Strains with Haze or Thai in their names typically have sativa parentage.

Meanwhile, *Cannabis indica* reigns supreme in bud and resin production, making it sought after for commercial production. This cannabis plant is short and strong (with dense resin-filled buds), because it is native to high mountain ranges (like the Hindu Kush mountain range in central Asia), where it needs protection from high winds, low temperatures, and strong UV rays. Its color is often deep green and even purple. The leaf blades are wide, and all are similar in length, width, and shape. Any strain with the name Kush in it likely has indica parentage.

CONVENTIONAL VS. ORGANIC

Conventional farming allows for the use of additives, pesticides, and herbicides. Technically, there isn't an organic standard for cannabis because organic products haven't been tested on cannabis. Every state deals with organic and nonorganic standards for cannabis differently. Regulated states test for illegal pesticides, molds, and bacteria before approving a product for sale.

Cannabis Products

When folks talk about the green rush (think: cannabis gold rush), it isn't just growing operations and dispensary shops sprouting up. It's also about the enormous range of products (both equipment and consumables) that have exploded in volume and variety. You are no longer bound to just bud. (Well, you kind of are.) While everything comes from the cannabis plant itself, there is now the knowledge and capability to

isolate certain aspects of the plant, like specific cannabinoids and terpenes, down to their pure forms.

Some will argue that because we don't yet know *all* of the aspects of this plant, we might not know what we are missing out on when we choose to isolate specific chemical compounds. It may be the *mix* of compounds (the entourage effect) that gives us the experience we value and seek. This can explain why a high-THC strain of flower will affect you differently from a water-soluble liquid dose of pure THC. One gives you THC *and* the other compounds of the plant; the other gives you just the THC.

Depending on your preferences or needs, you may only interact with certain types of cannabis in certain ways. Regardless, the variety of options now available is likely to impact you—from your experience at the dispensary to the conversations you have about pot with your friends.

FLOWER

The flower of the cannabis plant is what most of us are familiar with either from personal usage or from the entertainment world. Once the cannabis plant is ready for harvest, it's cut down, dried, and then cured before it gets packaged and distributed to your local dispensary. Flower can be in bud form (called flower, bud, nugget, green, grass, tree, sticky icky, herb . . . see page 18 for more terms for weed), or it can come as shake, where the bud has been broken apart until it resembles loose dried green herb. Dispensaries will often sell bags of shake, which dries out faster than buds but can still be useful.

EXTRACTS & CONCENTRATES

Whenever you extract cannabinoids and terpenes from the plant matter, using either a solvent or solventless process, you create extracts and concentrates. Solvents pass through the plant matter and collect the compounds; the solvent is then dissolved, leaving the desired cannabinoids and terpenes in a resinated form. This resin can take a number of forms, depending on the process used, but most extraction methods result in oils as the final product. How far the extraction or concentration process is taken will impact the potency and consistency of the end product. An initial extraction might result in a product with 75 percent THC. A concentration of that extracted product could bring that percentage to 98 percent.

Not all concentrates are the same, and it's important that you know what method of consumption works for the type of concentrate that you have. Many can be used in multiple ways, but not all, so be sure to check first. Dropping kief on your dab rig or putting tincture in your joint may not work out the way you want. (Though concentrate-enhanced bowls and joints do happen!)

Here are some common extracts and concentrates that you'll encounter in the wide world of pot products.

Kief It's like cannabis fairy dust! Kief is actually the plant's trichomes that have been knocked off the calyxes of the bud. If you get enough of them together, it is some wonderfully potent pot. Sprinkling a little on your joint or bowl is a great way to kick things up a notch. You'll find dispensaries selling kief, and many people collect their own from grinders and nug jars.

Hash One of the oldest forms of concentrated cannabis and consumed worldwide, hash comes in a number of forms and can be made in a number of ways, but most consist of collecting the resin (trichomes) from the plant and pressing them together.

Butane hash oil (BHO) This method uses butane (or propane in the case of PHO) as a solvent to pull the desired cannabinoids and terpenes out of the plant matter. The butane allows the extractor to get the desired compounds without also collecting undesired chemicals that are also found in the plant matter, like chlorophyll. The butane is then extracted out of the concentrated product. Done right, BHO is great. Done wrong, it can be both dangerous to make and a health risk. Be smart and only use products from reputable extractors.

CO$_2$ Oil The solvent supercritical carbon dioxide is used to make what is called a CO$_2$ oil. The CO$_2$ is a more natural solvent than some other methods used, making it more desirable for some.

RSO (Rick Simpson Oil/Phoenix Tears) Made by using an ethanol extraction method, RSO is a sworn-by supplement that can be ingested or applied to the skin.

RESINS

The collection of resin starts with the flower itself (living or dried) and uses various methods to pull the trichomes off the plant matter. These are then pressed together to create a resin. Making resin can be as simple as rubbing your hands on a live plant and then rubbing your hands together to the more complex process of using dry ice and mesh bags or a 4-ton press. Depending on how you make it, here are some of its names: charas, hashish, hash, shira, gara, water hash, or bubble hash. Resins and hash are usually added to joints, spliffs, and tobacco or smoked out of bowls and hookahs.

Live resin The freshest of the fresh, live resin is like consuming the live plant. The plant is flash-frozen immediately after being cut, and it's kept frozen throughout the extraction process. The end result is a product that ranges from a saplike consistency to a hard shatter (glasslike/candylike consistency). If you really want to taste your cannabis, vaporizing live resin is the way to go.

Rosin A supereasy way to get concentrate quickly, rosin is made by using a low-heat press to squeeze out the resinated cannabis from the flower. Folks that take rosin seriously have their own heavyweight presses, but parchment paper and a hair straightener are all you really need to make it.

Shatter A solid concentrate, shatter has a glass or hard candy–like consistency.

Crumble This is a solid concentrate with a graham cracker–like consistency.

Budder/wax A solid concentrate, budder/wax is formed when the plant fat isn't fully removed during the extraction process, so the consistency is a more pliable product.

Distillate Creating distillate results in a cannabis oil that is as clean as possible. There may be a range of compounds present, but no waxes, triglycerides, or chlorophyll remain after the extraction or concentration process.

Isolate When you isolate, you break down the cannabis to one particular compound. This takes the concentration process the farthest and can result in a product that is 100 percent pure THC, CBD, limonene, myrcene or other cannabinoid or terpene.

Tincture A tincture is made with cannabis-infused alcohol. Prior to 1911, when cannabis was a frequently used medicine, using tinctures was common. Tinctures are easy to measure and easy to take, either by adding them to a beverage, to raw or cold foods, or to foods that have been cooked. Alternatively, placing a drop or two under your tongue is a quick and easy way to take a tincture. Sublingually, the cannabinoids and terpenes will enter your system faster, and you can feel the effects as soon as fifteen minutes later. If you apply a tincture to food or drink, it will be metabolized by your liver and be more like an edible experience. Properly made and stored, tinctures can last for years.

ALREADY INFUSED

You can find all kinds of products on the market that are already infused with cannabis. From butters and oils to use in cooking, to snacks, nut spreads, chews, gummies, honey, and even salt and sugar. There are premade drinks and drink mixes that range in potency, allowing you to pace yourself or to consume your entire dose in one sip.

A HEALTH NOTE ABOUT CONCENTRATES

Since concentrates are new, it's important to pay attention to how they are made and what (if anything) is being added to them. The diluting agents used can be irritants for some people. Coconut oil is safe for edibles and salves, but it's bad to atomize and vaporize. Additives found in prefills are still considered a concern from a health standpoint. Don't be afraid to ask questions about how the product you're purchasing or being offered was made and whether anything was added to it.

TOPICALS & TRANSDERMALS

From Rescue Rub to Rick Simpson Oil and transdermal gel pens to cannabinoid-specific patches, transdermals are a very approachable way to use cannabis. Don't be surprised if you see them offered at a friend's home or even consistently kept in a bud bar as an option for those not wanting to eat or inhale.

The Chemistry of Cannabis

I worked with cannabis educator and consultant Emma Chasen to better understand the science behind cannabis and how it affects the human body. There are hundreds of natural chemical compounds in cannabis that can influence how it will affect you. The most common natural chemical compounds in cannabis are cannabinoids and terpenes.

THC (tetrahydrocannabinol) and CBD (cannabidiol) are two of the most commonly discussed cannabinoids, and there are more than 200 different types of terpenes found in cannabis. When the information is available, you want to be paying attention to the type and potency of the cannabinoids and terpenes that are dominant in the products you're buying. This will help you to target your experiences with cannabis. In legalized states with regulatory systems, all of the cannabis you purchase will have been lab tested for these compounds, making it easier to learn about and tailor your experience.

Emma Chasen describes the difference between cannabinoids and terpenes with this great metaphor: "Cannabinoids and terpenes are like your car. The cannabinoids are like the engine; they get everything going and determine how much power is behind the experience. Terpenes are like the steering wheel; they determine the direction the car is going."

A strain that is mild in THC (15 percent) won't give you a very powerful high, but if it has the terpene limonene in it, you're likely to have an uplifting experience, because limonene boosts your serotonin and dopamine levels. The combination would likely give you a light, happy high. Whereas if that same 15 percent THC is coupled with the terpenes linalool and humulene (which have more sedative effects), you're likely to feel sleepy but maybe not necessarily knocked out, since the THC content is still low. Let's explore cannabinoids and terpenes a bit more.

CANNABINOIDS

Cannabinoids are one type of chemical compound found within the cannabis plant. Of the 113 known cannabis cannabinoids, THC and CBD are the most widely known and sought after. The potency (usually 15 to 30 percent for flower and 70 to 98 percent for extracts and concentrates) along with the cannabinoids and terpenes present will help determine how the consumer actually experiences the cannabis. You could think of this in much the same way as evaluating the alcohol percentage and tasting notes for alcohol.

Different cannabinoids can have different effects on our bodies and, depending on whether they are raw, heated, or aged, their chemical formulation will change, thus changing their effect. For example, just from aging and being exposed to air and light, a dried cannabis flower's Delta 9 THC turns into CBN (cannabinol), which is a much more sedative cannabinoid. Take note, these effects are all real possibilities, but you have to consider the fact that each person is different.

Depending on the way you consume your cannabis, you could be getting more or less out of the cannabinoid that you're targeting. For example, THC that is activated at around 315°F can help reduce the amount of pressure in your eyes (a key goal for those with glaucoma), but if your vape pen is heating above 450°F or you're dabbing at 710°F (a favored number of the dab community because it spells OIL upside down), you're overheating the desired cannabinoid beyond its optimum activation temperature. It will still give you other effects, but it may have less impact on your intended goal.

Cannabinoids can also affect each other. While most cannabinoids are psychoactive because they interact with the brain, they don't all have the same effects and can sometimes counteract each other. When CBD is present with THC, it tones down the effects of the THC. If you're uncomfortably high and feeling anxious, consuming CBD will help to counteract the effects of the THC. You can find blended strains and products that have a range of THC to CBD ratios, which can help offer a balance.

Cannabinoids, while they engage with CB1 receptors (see page 36), have a low-binding affinity for them. What they really love is working with serotonin and dopamine receptors that modulate pain, temperature sensation, and homeostasis. And that is why THC and CBD can have such mood-elevating effects, since those are the receptors they gravitate toward.

Here are descriptions of three cannabinoids and the effects they can have on the body.

- **THC** relieves pain and symptoms of depression, reduces nausea and vomiting, suppresses muscle spasms, stimulates appetite, slows nervous system degeneration, and reduces eye pressure.

- **CBD** relieves pain and symptoms of depression, slows bacteria growth, reduces blood sugar as well as nausea and vomiting, seizures and convulsions, anxiety, and inflammation. CBD inhibits cancer cell growth, suppresses muscle spasms, stimulates bone growth, and slows nervous system degeneration.

- **CBN** relieves pain, aids sleep, and suppresses muscle spasms.

TERPENES

Terpenes are organic aromatic chemical compounds found in all plants, defining tastes and aromas. They affect your experience with each plant, as well as with each strain of cannabis. They are the same compounds that we extract to create essential oils—the terpene linalool, for example, is the principal compound responsible for the association between lavender and a sense of calm. The reason we associate pine with uplifting, happy, clean, focused feelings is because of the terpene pinene, which is found in pine needles. The cannabis strain Jack Herer has a strong piney smell to it due to its higher quantities of pinene. One of the things that pinene is known for is being a bronchial dilator, which means it helps open up our airways, so we can breathe more easily. More oxygen gives us humans a fresh, focused feeling. So when you vape Jack Herer, you feel clear, focused, and uplifted in the same way that the smell of pine makes us feel, clean, fresh, and invigorated. (That pinene is a sweet little terp!)

Here are descriptions of three terpenes and the effects they can have on the body.

- **Limonene** is found in citrus fruits and has a strong citrus aroma that is energizing to the brain. It elevates mood by engaging with our serotonin receptors and can help reduce anxiety.

- **Linalool** has a sweet, floral aroma and is found in lavender. It has a relaxing effect and can reduce anxiety. Relaxing as it is, linalool can also uplift your mood.

- **Myrcene** is the most common terpene found in cannabis, and it is also found in hops. It has a sweet, earthy aroma. Strains testing at over 0.5 percent myrcene will relax you; under 0.5 percent will uplift you. This terpene also helps enhance the effects of THC.

CANNABINOID AND TERPENE ACTIVATION TEMPERATURES

As mentioned on page 33, temperature matters in terms of optimizing your cannabis experience. Do your research (and personal experimenting) but here is a general overview of what different cannabinoids and terpenes can aid with if consumed at certain activation temperatures. Vape devices, electronic nail dab setups, and your oven or a cooking thermometer are all ways to consume or cook consumable cannabis and succeed in hitting an activation temperature. Here are some cannabinoid and terpene activation temperatures and effects courtesy of Goldleaf.

a-Pinene at 311ºF: analgesic, antiasthmatic, anti-inflammatory

a-Terpineol at 423ºF: antibacterial, anti-insomnia, immunostimulant

CBD at 356ºF: analgesic, antibacterial, antidepressant, antidiabetic, antiemetic, antiepileptic, anti-inflammatory, antiproliferative, antipsychotic, sedative, antianxiolytic, bone stimulant, neuro-protactive

CBN at 365ºF: analgesic, anti-insomnia, antispasmotic

Linalool at 388ºF: analgesic, antiepileptic, anti-insomnia, antiproliferative, antipsychotic, anxiolytic, sedative

Myrcene at 334ºF: analgesic, antidepressant, anti-inflammatory, antipsychotic, antispasmotic, enhances the effects of THC, immunostimulant, sedative

THC at 315ºF: analgesic, antibacterial, antidepressant, antiemetic, antispasmotic, appetite stimulant, neuroprotactive, reduces intraocular eye pressure

THCa at 220ºF: anti-inflammatory, antiproliferative, antispasmodic

The Human Body & Cannabis

"Like oil to the tin man, cannabis is to the human body."

—Emma Chasen

Understanding how cannabis works in the body and why we feel the effects that we do can give us a lot more choice and control regarding our engagement with it.

The endogenous cannabinoid system (endocannabinoid system) is a physiological system in humans (and other animals) composed of cannabinoid receptors (the CB1 and CB2) and cannabinoid-signaling molecules. These receptors are meant to receive cannabinoids from cannabis as well as cannabinoid-like compounds found in other plants (like rosemary, black truffles, and echinacea). It has the ability to influence many of our bodies' systems (sleep, appetite, immune function, mood, and pain) and, when engaged, helps to keep our physiological systems running smoothly.

It's worth noting that THC and CBD bind differently from one another with the CB1 receptor. THC can bind right away, but CBD needs THC to bind first in order to be able to bind. The THC signals the CB1 receptor to create a landing site for the CBD. CBD can still bind to fifteen other receptors on its own and still have positive effects. But in order for it to be powerfully effective, CBD needs THC.

THE PHYSIOLOGY OF GETTING HIGH

Our brains have a blood-brain barrier that functions like a sieve around the brain, keeping out large, potentially toxic chemical compounds. What this barrier allows in are fat-soluble compounds like those found in cannabis. The larger the compound, the harder it is to cross the blood-brain barrier. Terpenes are tiny little compounds, so they can pass through easily. Our brain wants to receive them. They signal to our bodies whether we should engage with whatever those terpenes are coming from.

Because cannabinoids are often large, clunky compounds, they can't pass through the blood-brain barrier as easily. When terpenes and cannabinoids are together (in the flower or concentrates that you consume), the terpenes help the cannabinoids get across the barrier. This allows more of the cannabinoids to enter your system and increases the effects of both compounds on your body.

When you smoke or vape, you consume THC in what's known as the Delta 9 THC molecule, which is a large molecule. When inhaled, this compound isn't getting into your brain easily because of its size and because if you are combusting, you are likely burning off many of the terpenes that can help it get across the blood-brain barrier.

When you eat an edible of the same strain, the Delta 9 THC is metabolized and processed in your liver. This metabolization causes the Delta 9 THC to transform and become 11-hydroxy THC, which is a much smaller cannabinoid. When 11-hydroxy THC heads to the brain, not only does it have an easier time crossing the barrier, it also binds to the brain's receptors better. This is why edibles can be more intense than smoking or vaping and take longer to have an effect.

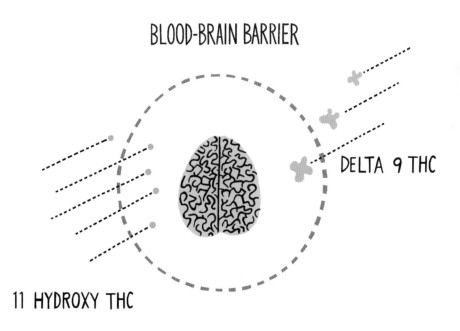

BLOOD-BRAIN BARRIER

DELTA 9 THC

11 HYDROXY THC

While it's harder to control the temperature from a flame, certain smoke and vape devices can give you greater precision over temperature control and this can make a difference to your experience. When you heat your cannabis above 500°F, you're burning off a lot of the delicate terpene compounds that can assist you in receiving your desired high and health benefits from cannabis. Paying attention to temperature will help you maximize and control your experience. It's worth noting, too, that the chemical compounds in cannabis do not interact with the part of the brain stem that regulates cardiopulmonary functions. (Read this as: cannabis can't shut down your heart or lungs.)

Cannabis Strains

Most folks refer to strains when talking about the different types of cannabis plants that we consume: White Widow, Strawberry Cough, Maui Wowie, GSC, Durban Poison, and so on. There are literally thousands of varieties of cannabis, and they have been crossbred and hybridized into a dizzying matrix of Mary Jane. From a scientific standpoint, the term *strain* is usually associated with bacteria. Horticulturally speaking, strains are the types and varieties of the cannabis plant.

STRAIN NAMES

Cannabis strains have all kinds of names and reasons for those names. A strain name doesn't always reflect the experience you will have with that particular strain. Psycho, for example, won't necessarily make you feel psycho. And not all strains that share a name end up having the same effects: not all Durban Poisons will hit you the same way. While this is not something to be overly concerned with, it's good to be aware of it.

Strain names are so much fun, but here's why there's so much inaccuracy: any grower can name a batch she is growing with whatever name she chooses, making, for myriad reasons, for the name that you see in the store.

Strain names can be chosen based on some strong strain lines whose lineage has lasted, on the cultivators themselves, or on the flower's color, smell, taste, effect, or area of origin. Often the strain's parent names are combined in the "child name," such as with Blue Haze, which is Blue Dream crossed with Super Silver Haze. Names can even be poetic, like the Oregon-based grow operation Raven Grass's Frida strain. It's a cross between ACDC (a CBD-dominant strain that promotes pain relief) and Whitaker Blues (an indica-dominant strain with relaxing, euphoric effects). The combination is likely to help ease pain while getting you into a happy, creative space. Thus the inspiration to name the strain Frida after Frida Kahlo, the twentieth-century Mexican artist who channeled pain into her painting. Clever, right? Marketing and customer appeal also drive names (and sometimes inaccuracies). Leafly.com and Phylos Bioscience are useful sources for strain lineages, genetics, and even backstories. Grab your vape pen and enjoy searching . . . for a few hours.

STRAINS & THEIR EFFECTS

Many dispensaries, companies, and friends will talk about sativas being uplifting and euphoric (social) and indicas giving a relaxed and sedative feel (in-da-couch); hybrids can be any combination. These days, there's a lot of discussion around moving the focus and language away from associating the effects of a given strain with the physical characteristics of the plant; this is what the words *indica* and *sativa* are referring to. It's wise to be open to shifting your frame of reference and to do your research about strains. Remember: it's the combination of chemical compounds in the plant that will determine your experience, not the physical characteristics of how the plant grows and looks, or even its name.

When you go into a dispensary or are asking someone about their homegrown, talking about the effects of a strain is the best way to determine if you'd like that particular variety of cannabis. Describe what you're looking to feel (or avoid) when you're seeking a strain at a dispensary and keep an open mind to what the budtender suggests. Smelling is also a great test. You'll either be drawn to a strain by its scent—oh, those terpenes!—or you won't.

Positive-effect key words: relaxed, happy, sleepy, uplifted, euphoric, creative, hungry, focused, energetic, motivated

Negative-effect key words: dry mouth, dry eyes, dizziness, anxiety, paranoia, drowsiness

"I want a strain that gives me focus but keeps me relaxed."

"I need a sleep aid that also relieves pain."

"I want a giggly-daytime high that I can be social on!"

Learning which cannabinoid and terpene combinations often result in these effects can help you better understand the cannabis you purchase and consume. Knowledge is power, and flower power is awesome!

To give you an idea of how different potencies and cannabinoid-terpene combinations might affect you, here are two strain snapshots, courtesy of Emma Chasen.

STRAIN NAME: CRITICAL MASS

THC: 15 percent **CBD:** 15 percent

Myrcene: Found in most cultivars (varieties); when combined with THC and CBD, it helps to relax the body.

a-Pinene: Found in pine needles, it has that fresh piney flavor and aroma. It is a bronchodilator, allowing your airway and lungs to open/deepen. Your brain and body connect pinene with a clean, clear sensation due to the increased concentration of oxygen in the blood/tissues.

Most likely effect: Relaxing body sensation (pain relief!), coupled with a clear, positive, and energized mental state.

STRAIN NAME: COOKIES & CREAM

THC: 24 to 28 percent **CBD:** 0 to 1 percent

Myrcene: Our friend is back (see above), but this time the combination has a different result.

b-Caryophyllene: Found in black pepper, cloves, and cinnamon, it binds to our CB2 endocannabinoid receptors, which, when engaged, do not signal for psychoactive responses but rather for pain relief and body relaxation. It also has measurable antianxiety properties.

Most likely effect: Deep relaxation of both the body and mind.

CANNABIS & YOU

CHAPTER 3

Best buds.

.

Enjoying cannabis is a personal choice, and like all
personal choices, you get to decide if and how it fits
into your life. For some people, cannabis is only medicinal; for others, their purpose can range from using
it as a creative aid or motivational aid, to a dietary
supplement, social lubricant, medicine, or therapy.
Much like our dietary preferences, our pot preferences
will be personal and will likely change over time. As
cannabis becomes more broadly legalized, it's worth
taking a minute to think about your own purpose(s) for
engaging with it. This can prevent getting caught in an
awkward situation as well as increase your confidence
in communicating your opinions and thoughts on
cannabis. Understanding your purpose, means, and
preferences for engaging with (or avoiding) cannabis
will allow you to be reflective, polite, and responsible
about your consumption and conversations around
and with family, friends, and coworkers.

Privacy and discretion are a big part of etiquette in all areas of life. Who do you feel comfortable letting know that you use cannabis? Just because you might feel safe and even proud disclosing that you use it, you might not feel that way with everyone and it doesn't mean all cannabis consumers feel the same way. Pot is personal, and whether it's medicinal or not, you get to decide who knows what about you. Cannabis has spent decades being pigeonholed as a problem, and de-stigmatization takes time. Considering who you're willing to have in your cannabis life and who you'll be more reserved around will help you know how to conduct yourself in many situations.

Conversations About Cannabis

People talk and identify differently from one another when it comes to cannabis. One of the most respectful acts with which you can begin a conversation about cannabis is to pay attention to how someone identifies and the language they choose to use. You don't have to adopt their ideas or agree with them, but using reflective language when speaking with them about their use is considerate. Both parties should be aiming to do so.

I fully admit that when I'm asked about what's new in etiquette and I excitedly share this book topic, I get disheartened when the response is, "Does that even exist?" or "Oh yeah, stoners need it badly." I know that not everyone supports the use of cannabis, but as an etiquette expert, it was clear that I had to encourage building relationships and broadening perspectives around cannabis while being respectful, especially if that's the consideration and respect I was hoping for from others.

What is a win in the cannabis conversation department? Talking with someone who isn't pro-cannabis and walking away feeling like you were understood and respected, and that you understood and respected their point of view. It often takes patience from both parties and a willingness to listen to each other's experience without assuming it needs to be your experience.

"I'll take a hit if something's being passed around."

"It's my medicine and it helps my creativity."

"I'm done with tree; it's dabs all the way."

HOW TO BE A GOOD CANNABIS AMBASSADOR

While you can't control the disparaging comments or negative attitudes of others, you can still be a good ambassador for the cannabis community. While you are but one perspective, yours matters and communicating it well is the first step.

Speak from a personal perspective. People can argue facts, but it's tougher for them to argue or be upset if you're sharing your experience. "My experience with pot has been really positive. I like it because . . ." When your approach doesn't accuse others and represents your own experience, it's hard for someone to argue or be dismissive of it without being rude directly toward you.

Break down stereotypes slowly and without judgment. Recognizing that a stereotype is real is okay, but you can always add your own perspective to help change the image from only being a stereotype: "Yeah, Cheech and Chong are classic, but most of the people I get high with don't fit that 1970s stoner image." Or, you can counter comments about stereotypical stoners with interest rather than disdain. "Most of the people I know who smoke weed, you'd never know they were high just from talking to them."

Be realistic. While many cannabis consumers are balanced and responsible with their usage, cannabis can be problematic for some. It's important to recognize that not everyone's experience will be rosy. The subject of alcohol is a familiar example to turn to when you begin a conversation on responsibility, substances, and medical choices.

Broaden horizons. Offering up examples of lesser-known qualities or uses of cannabis is a great way to open up people's minds. "Did you know some people don't even get a foggy-head high when they use it?" Many people have no idea how broad the reasons for engaging with cannabis are, and many folks can more easily change their perspectives when they see it's not about being baked out of your gourd all day long.

Agree to disagree. If someone is really not going to accept that you or others should have the right to use cannabis, it's usually best to let it go. Even this can be the act of a good communicator. "I wish we could be on the same page, but I think for now, we see this subject differently" is a stronger, more respectful perspective to close the conversation with than "You're wrong!" or "Way to be ignorant . . . real great . . . go you."

POT PREFERENCES

It's perfectly okay to have preferences about your consumption, whether it's preferring glass to paper for smoking or using only solvent-less extracts. But *how* you handle preferences is where etiquette comes in. As with dietary preferences, it's okay to ask questions about the products you're being offered. It's also okay to decline because the method or product being offered to you isn't one you enjoy. Asking to ask is always a good place to start: "May I ask where you got it?" "May I ask what strain it is?" Cannabis experiences are personal, so it's always important to respect someone's choices for their own usage.

In order to be delicate and not come off as snobbish or demanding, you must always remain cool about it. No pouting if your host doesn't have what you like. Act as if it doesn't even matter that you can't or won't partake; you're there to enjoy the company of others. And certainly abandon any lofty attitudes about your preferences being the right ones or better than what's being offered. Be smart with your words and tone so as not to offend.

Things to say

- "I'd love some. I tend to stay away from solvents, though. Do you happen to know how it was extracted?"

- "I'm good for now but thank you for offering."

- "You know I just never got into spliffs, but thank you."

Things not to say

- "Flower is just so pedestrian."

- "Added flavorings make that oil basically poison if you think about it."

- "I hate when tobacco's mixed in . . . but you go right ahead."

Cannabis & Boundaries

Whether your boundaries are for you alone, you and your partner, or you and your children, boundaries regarding cannabis should be set. It's important to be able to navigate these conversations with respect and consideration for all involved. When it comes to protecting personal boundaries, some people have the grace and tact to gather the information they need to make decisions for themselves without judging others. But not everyone is so tactful.

It can be tempting to put a hand in the face of a person asking about your usage or if cannabis is kept in your home. How dare they?! But if you can muster your higher self, take a breath and realize that this person is seeking information. (Even if they are not the most tactful about acquiring it, *you* can still be graceful about the situation.)

For example, let's say that Melissa says to Bree, "I'm thrilled the boys want to do a playdate, but I know you smoke pot, so I have to ask if there's pot in your home and if so, how is it stored for me to feel safe about Connor playing at your house." This was *not* the polite way for Melissa to broach the subject. Instead, explaining that she has a cannabis boundary and asking permission to ask some questions would have been better (and something Melissa may want to get comfortable doing—whether the other parent has mentioned cannabis or not—if her boundary is firm). In situations like this, take a deep breath and remind yourself that people get awkward when they are nervous or protective. Give her the benefit of the doubt.

Bree can either choose to entertain some of Melissa's concerns and share what she wishes to with her or she can offer to have the kids play at Melissa's house or at another location. Rather than put the focus only onto Melissa's lack of tact and Bree's rights to privacy and to keep cannabis in her home, the conversation can be directed to a solution that lets the kids play together and makes the parents feel comfortable. (Take note, if you do need to draw the line at someone making a comment, especially about your medicinal consumption, a simple "I'm not comfortable sharing my medical information. Let's have the boys play at the park or your house" should work.)

EXPOSURE

Here are three points to consider when it comes to exposing someone else's or your own cannabis consumption.

1. **Loose lips.** Don't "out" someone's cannabis habits to anyone. It's not your place, and while it usually happens in the most innocent of ways—true *oops* moments—it can really be an issue for the person being outed. If a friend tells you that their boss, mother-in-law, client, or kid's teacher doesn't know about their cannabis use and they'd like it to stay that way, be aware when encountering these folks not to make comments on the subject unless your friend does first.

2. **Personal exposure.** Be in control of your own image. Take care with the pictures, posts, and comments that you make online. If a friend makes a reference or posts a picture you're not comfortable with, it's okay to ask them to take it down. Sample language: "Hey, I had a great time Friday night, but would you be willing to take down that photo of me hitting the bong? I'm pretty careful about keeping my cannabis use offline. I'd really appreciate it."

3. **Judgment day.** Most people seem to live and let live. Unfortunately, the reality is that no matter how comfortable you are with cannabis, there are folks who may not be, and they may judge you for your usage. You can choose to engage calmly and be a good cannabis ambassador or you can choose to walk away and let the other person live in his world, while you enjoy cannabis in yours. At the Emily Post Institute, we talk a lot about taking the high road when it comes to etiquette. Don't stoop to someone else's level of judgment. Whether it's out loud or just a thought, take a moment and recognize that you both exist and that you have the right to have different viewpoints on the matter.

FIVE STEPS TO HANDLING DIFFICULT CANNABIS CONVERSATIONS

So you've reached that totally awkward moment when you realize that your relative, friend, or coworker is not pro-cannabis. Sadly, some friendships, family relationships, and working situations have been divided by this subject—with both enjoyers and abstainers choosing to draw the line. We can all understand that we have different opinions and reasons for those opinions, but what the heck do you do when you've just admitted to your friend that you enjoy ganja and he says he's totally not okay with that?

1. **Go basic.** State that you value his friendship and that you want to preserve it despite your differences of opinions.

2. **Can we be friends?** Ask if he is still willing to be friends. (For real, drama queen? For real.) People have all kinds of reasons for not wanting to associate with cannabis; it may have little to do with you and your personal choice and more to do with him and his. Start from a place of understanding if he doesn't want to be friends.

3. **Assess the degree of difficulty.** Understand his boundaries. Ask whether he can be around you when you consume or if he'd prefer your time together to be weed-free.

4. **Now it's your turn.** Once you understand your friend's comfort levels and needs, decide if you're willing to meet them. By identifying the level of engagement your friendship can have regarding cannabis, you can figure out what works for you.

5. **Find ways to make it work.** Maybe you're one-on-one friends, and you choose not to be high around him because that's easy for you to do. Maybe he's fine with coming to any party you host but just wants a heads-up if it'll be a toke fest. Maybe you only hang at his house. There are many options here, but the point is, if you don't talk about it together, you might lose the friendship.

For how far cannabis has come, especially in recent years, it's still a confusing and sometimes uncomfortable topic for some. Being aware, patient, and understanding is the key to navigating any awkward cannabis conversations.

Weed & Work

When it comes to cannabis and the time clock, the rules and expectations at noncannabis industry companies can vary greatly. Some companies might embrace the ability to include cannabis at company events, while others might have policies that require drug testing. When cannabis is prohibited, it's fairly cut and dry. But as states legalize (both medicinal and adult usage), companies have to make decisions about cannabis and work. For employees at companies that haven't set a policy, you'll have to make decisions for yourself, based on whether or not it would be appropriate to hit your vape on a coffee break or discuss CBD with a coworker.

While the era of the martini lunch has long gone from the average work setting, weed and work is one place where the alcohol precedent might not hold, and we find ourselves in new territory. Cannabis, unlike alcohol, can be someone's daily supplement or medication, making it virtually impossible for them not to have consumed before or during an average workday. It will be interesting to see what kinds of policies companies set as legalization moves forward. As with all personal issues in the workplace, it's an area in which it's best to use your best judgment and knowledge of your company's culture and policies.

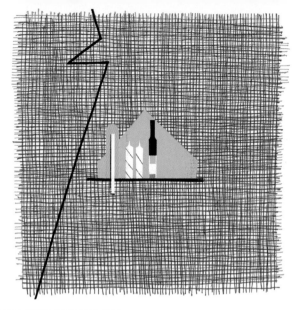

WITHIN THE INDUSTRY

Of the interesting topics that arise when it comes to weed and work within the cannabis industry, the two main points I hear frequently are in regard to respecting consumption boundaries while on the clock and staying humble.

If you are having a business meeting to learn about someone's consumable products (and you haven't planned on sampling), it's okay to turn down an offer to try the product on the spot. "Thank you. I'd love to try some a little later once we've completed our business" or "I'd love to take some with me to try at home." Since most folks are very conscious about personal consumption choices, you shouldn't have to give a reason beyond this.

There is new ground being broken daily in the world of cannabis. Whether it's new research or methods or products or experiences, the world of cannabis is booming, and it's okay that our knowledge is evolving and changing as well. As we learn, it's important to remember that others are learning, too. Being humble and kind when sharing our knowledge will get us much further as a culture than arrogance and smugness. There is a lot of encouragement to embrace the cannabis industry as a community that will rise together rather than compete viciously.

Many budtenders and growers who have to get certified or permitted to work in the cannabis industry are not willing to have their jobs compromised because their friends are choosing to be casual about their consumption and breaking the law. A number of budtenders I spoke to mentioned feeling confident in speaking up, especially in the case of travel. For example, in Colorado, dispensary canisters cannot be open in a car and must be out of arm's reach from the driver. If a friend isn't transporting their cannabis properly in the car, you might say, "Hey, can we put this away? I can't risk my dispensary badge [card/license]." A good friend will happily oblige.

Medicinal Cannabis

The body is built to receive cannabinoids and terpenes, and humans have used cannabis as a medicine for thousands of years. Even now, researchers are exploring and learning new ways that cannabis can benefit the mind and body. Despite the Schedule I drug classification of cannabis, many states have legalized medicinal programs. It's important to realize that medicinal cannabis varies in both quality and allowance state by state, and it can be different from recreational or adult-use products. Some states only allow certain consumption methods and certain products for medicinal cannabis. Dosage is also sometimes controlled. But the biggest thing to remember when it comes to cannabis as a medicine: medical information is confidential and private.

IDENTITY

Some medicinal users identify as patients, and others don't. Some choose to use cannabis for their health benefit but don't consider that usage medicinal. For some, the medicinal usage to heal an injury or tackle a disease or condition is temporary. Others believe that all usage is medicinal. Some folks use it as a form of therapy. Whether it's one of these perspectives or a mix of them, the etiquette is to respect and not negatively comment on how someone chooses to identify.

Many medicinal consumers struggle with the stoner stigmas. Some avoid the heavier psychoactive effects of cannabis altogether and resent being labeled or judged negatively for choosing cannabis to alleviate their symptoms. No matter how you identify as a medicinal cannabis consumer, your medical choices are private and should be respected as such. If anyone pushes you for comment, you may politely let them know, "I'm not comfortable discussing my medical life at the moment."

If someone has discussed their medicinal usage with you, there are two things to consider. First, reflect the language they use by using it as well when speaking with them. Second, you should not share your knowledge of their use with others. If you think this person's story might help someone else you know, always ask permission to share it before doing so. Sharing can be useful, but "Oh yeah, Bill uses it as one of his cancer treatments" should not be tossed around casually or without permission.

NO PINCHING

Don't ask a medicinal patient if you can have some of his medicinal cannabis. In most states, he is not allowed to give it to you, and he could lose his medical card if he is caught. It's not worth the risk, and while most patients have a friendly, polite response ready to go ("Sorry, I can't give it to anyone or I lose my card"), don't put him in the position of having to use it.

THE 420-
FRIENDLY
HOUSEHOLD

CHAPTER 4

You and your cannabis are welcome here.

In your own home, you decide how cannabis is handled when it comes to living with others and inviting guests over. There are many places where good forethought and higher etiquette can help smooth the way to a happy 420-friendly home for all.

Roommates & Reefer

Depending on how you use cannabis, the effect on your roommates can be either minimal or a real issue. Whether you are the one moving in or you're the current tenant, ask about cannabis consumption upfront. Seriously. If ganja is a daily or even regular part of your life and you are deciding on or even considering living with someone, it's imperative to disclose your habits and comfort levels. For your sake and theirs, be open and honest. As long as you each put your perspective on the table, you'll be able to figure out the rest before you make a commitment to signing a lease.

HOUSE PREFERENCES

How households choose to be 420 friendly varies. From the type of usage allowed to standards around the product and equipment being used—the when, where, and by whom—each home has its own style and boundaries. I was surprised to find so many "no indoor combustion" households in legalized states. Most hosts were fine with vapor, but smoke was not welcome indoors. You'll also want to check with your building or homeowner's association about smoking rules.

Here are some topics to consider when thinking about how cannabis is consumed in your home:

- Methods of use indoors and outdoors
- Rooms or outside areas designated for consumption
- Hours of the day
- Houseguests and visitors
- House stashes
- Equipment usage
- Pinching

- Ashing

- Labeling

- Discarding

The list could go on, but making decisions together around some of these topics can help you avoid frustration on the home front.

THE HOUSE STASH

Many households keep a communal house stash for residents and visitors. Folks add to it and take from it when they can and want to, but it's important to decide on some household courtesies. Whether these are casual or more detailed will vary, depending on everyone's preferences, but having the conversation up front will head off potential awkwardness down the line about refilling, labeling, or sharing the house stash. House stash rules might include that you need to replace what you take or that all houseguest gifted weed goes into the house stash.

"Any weed that is brought as a hosting gift is put in the house stash."

"The house stash is fair game, but special strains are kept in our bedrooms."

"We don't have a house stash; people just pinch from each other."

PINCHING

Taking a pinch of someone's weed without asking (pinching) is not as common as it once was in areas where weed is legal and dispensaries are accessible. Still, convenience can lead anyone to pinch some from their roommate, knowing they will "get 'em back later." Some folks are cool with pinching; others are not. If you don't keep a communal pot, it's best to ask so that you can know whether it's an okay move when you're in a . . . pinch.

WHOSE BUD BELONGS TO WHOM?

Labeling your cannabis is definitely considered higher roommate etiquette. Whether it's to identify it as yours or to make it known that it's a cannabis product, label items clearly. Most people know what their nug jar looks like, but if you and your roommates are all prone to Mason jars, it's not a bad idea to find some form of distinction between them. On the flip side, pay attention to what you're taking nugget or concentrate from. With people purchasing the same products from the same neighborhood dispensary, it's easy to grab your roommate's dispensary canister instead of yours.

WHO, WHAT, WHEN, WHERE & HOW?

Who can consume what, when, where, and how are the basic questions you have to answer when figuring out the rules of roasting or vaping at home. You'll want to discuss where cannabis can be used and how. While edibles and transdermals don't really affect others occupying the same space (unless accidentally consumed or used), smoke and sometimes vapor can impact any member of the house.

Even once you have established household norms, it never hurts to double-check. A simple "Are you cool with this?" or "Want me to open a window?" will suffice if your roommate isn't partaking and you want to consume. Read the room—even when it's just the two of you, choose a method that makes sense for the moment (for example, using a loud consumption method—hello, blowtorch!—during a movie is not thoughtful to those around you). A general check-in every now and again is always a good idea, especially in the early days of a roommate relationship.

EQUIPMENT STORAGE & USE

Equipment sharing and use can sometimes be more of an issue than pinching product. Gorgeous smoking pieces, intricate rigs, and expensive vaporizers can quickly become sore points in a household if they aren't cared for or, worse yet, are broken beyond repair. Be realistic about how you'd feel if your favorite piece broke. It's okay to have pieces that are off limits—many dab rig owners will let only a few trusted dabbing friends use their prized rigs. It's equally okay to have standards and expectations around how pieces are used and cleaned. It's important to be respectful of your roommate's wishes and property.

When it comes to communal equipment, return house pieces to their places when you are finished using them and remember that just like the dishes, communal glass needs to be cleaned, and it may be a task to add to the proverbial chore wheel.

Contact Highs?

According to Ryan Vandrey, PhD, an associate professor of psychiatry and behavioral sciences at Johns Hopkins University School of Medicine, who coauthored a study on the effects of secondhand cannabis smoke, the contact high—and potential for THC to show up on a drug test—is real but only under *extreme* conditions.

Dr. Vandrey's study placed twelve adults ages eighteen to forty-five in a 10 by 13-foot chamber with no ventilation. Six participants were given ten joints to smoke for one hour; the other six were not given joints and did not smoke off the other joints. Researchers periodically tested the participants' cognition and gave them urine tests. Only after an hour, when the smoke was so thick that it burned peoples' eyes, did a urine drug test reveal THC in a nonsmoker's urine. A positive THC result showed up in one nonsmoking participant on one of the multiple urine tests given. In terms of a contact high, participants who didn't smoke did feel a mild effect and demonstrated mild impairment on some standard cognitive performance measures. The six nonsmokers didn't feel like the six smokers did, but they did test as "different" from what you would consider a baseline.

Dr. Vandrey notes that frequent exposure to lesser amounts of secondhand cannabis smoke may be a different story. So if you're smoking a joint before bedtime every night and your partner is inhaling the secondhand smoke each night, that *may* create a different testing result. But if you are in a ventilated room at an average dinner party and you are only consuming secondhand smoke, you are not consuming potent enough secondhand smoke for a long enough period of time in large enough quantities to register on a standard urine drug test.

That said, regardless of their reasons, if someone is concerned about a contact high or drug test result, be courteous and open a window or consume in a different room or outside if possible. It's an easy solution for putting others at ease.

Hosting Houseguests

Depending on who is coming to stay, you may choose to change up your household routine or not. A host who combusts at home might choose to combust outside while her sister who doesn't comes to visit. Other hosts might choose to remove all cannabis-related material from the house while a "less than pro-cannabis" relative or friend comes to stay (not out of shame but out of consideration). Others will choose to be who they are and let guests know at the time the invitation is issued that "we are a 420-friendly home." The specific circumstances of each visit will likely dictate what you decide to do, but without making you uncomfortable in your own home, it's best to err on the side of making your guests feel comfortable. If there's any conflict between those two goals, most hosts (and guests) will suggest that the guest stay at a nearby hotel during the visit.

EXPLAIN EXPECTATIONS

While staying in Portland, Oregon, for book research, I was impressed at how casually and considerately all of my hosts (whether they were friends or AirBnB hosts) informed me of the household cannabis policy, requesting that combustion happen outdoors and that ashtrays be properly used. Be sure to inform your guests about where, when, and how you'd prefer cannabis to be consumed and disposed of in your house or on your property. Also take the time to let them know how you choose to enjoy cannabis at home. "We often have a bong out while watching TV. Please feel free to pack and hit it anytime you'd like."

THE GUEST CANNA-KIT

Jennifer Martin of Magnolia Road Cannabis Company set me up with the sweetest canna-kit upon my arrival at her home in Boulder, Colorado. It had a Stash Box vape pen and a couple of different types of oil cartridges, bottles of water, a mix of munchies (popcorn, jerky, nuts, chocolate, granola bars, and fruit), along with a note welcoming me. Providing herb for your guests' visit is up to you, your hosting style, and your budget. While you may be happy to take your guests to dispensaries so they can really get a great legalized experience, it's also thoughtful to have some flower (or concentrate) to give them upon arrival, so they can feel free to enjoy cannabis at their leisure. Remember to offer strain and effect information.

BEING A CANNABIS TOUR GUIDE

For guests coming in from out of state who are interested in the local cannabis scene, consider planning some trips to dispensaries that offer a more educational or boutique experience. This isn't because high-end dispensaries are the only polite way to engage with pot but rather because the store can be more comfortable and relatable for your guests. There are plenty of dispensaries that operate with a more casual appearance or staff that aren't interested in furthering your education.

Taking a guest (especially a newbie) to a shop where the space alone is something they might be familiar with can help make the less familiar experience of showing your ID multiple times and learning about strains and cannabis chemistry more inviting.

Grow tours, cannactivities like yoga classes and puff 'n' paints, cannabis parties, and educational events are all great ways to engage guests who are looking to explore the world of weed during their visit. (For more about cannactivities and weedcations, see pages 142 and 149.)

"The kids see me vape, but we don't combust herb around them."

"Everyone is asked to smoke/vape outside and encouraged to wash their hands when they come in."

"We taught our kids that this is for adults only. They see it consumed at our family gatherings."

Family

Much as with tobacco, firearms, alcohol, prescription drugs, sex, and many other topics, families—be they couples, couples with kids, or extended family living together—make choices regarding what they allow in their home and the level of exposure for particular family members.

Not all cannabis-friendly families are alike. The considerations for an all-adult family will be different from those for a family with underage members. Often for all-adult family living situations, the considerations default similarly to those for roommates. For families with underage members, some see exposure as a safety tactic and want their children to become familiar with what cannabis products, equipment, and supplies look like, in the same way that you would make it known to a child that the wine or beer in the house is for adults only or that certain household products are off limits until they are old enough to understand and execute proper use. Some families prefer to keep kids sheltered from cannabis.

Many parents make the amount-of-exposure decision based on the nature of their children. Are they (innocently or determinedly) curious? Are they aware of and respectful of boundaries set by adults? How old are they? It's common for parents to adjust their home life and usage habits depending on the ages of their children.

While the parents and families I spoke with all had different rules and expectations around cannabis, a few things were very consistent. Foremost among these is that respecting a family's personal choices and boundaries is important, even if those choices and boundaries do not reflect your own. Also, secondhand smoke is not healthy—anyone in the family who doesn't combust cannabis should not have to be exposed to cannabis smoke.

COMMON KID CONCERNS

You may encounter folks who have concerns about cannabis households and playdates. Here are three concerns that come up often:

- Is it in the house?

- Is it kept safely away?

- Is it used inside the home and if so, could the kids be exposed to it?

These are fair considerations and may or may not be deal breakers. You'll have to decide for yourself whether or not you're willing to entertain these questions and with whom. You may feel that your consumption is a private affair that you don't need to discuss, or you may be happy to chat with other parents about it. Here is some sample language for both scenarios:

- "My consumption is private, but I'm happy to have the kids play at the park (rec center, your house) instead if you're concerned about my house and safety."

- "I'm happy to talk with you about your concerns and then you can decide if we can do playdates at my house or if you'd rather the girls meet elsewhere."

Regarding Neighbors & Nugget

When it comes to smoke and aromas, your cannabis could affect your neighbors. Just as cigarette smokers should be able to enjoy their smoke on their own property while at the same time being mindful of where their smoke drifts, so, too, it is for cannabis smokers (and possibly backyard growers). Rather than stake your territory and make dividing lines about *your* yard, *your* balcony, or *your* rights, higher etiquette encourages you to recognize that you and your habits may have an effect on others and that it's okay to invite a bit of negotiation around that, up to a point.

If a neighbor is being rude and judgmental, you don't have to bend over backward to try to please them. But starting from a place of, "My goal is not to disrupt your enjoyment of your home or yard" is definitely your best chance at moving forward and building a good relationship.

Let the conversation come up organically (you don't have to Girl Scout it: *ding dong* "Hello, I'm Lizzie Post, and I smoke pot. If it ever bothers you, please feel free to let me know"). Instead, if you're on the balcony and they are on their balcony and you've got a blunt going, you can mention, "Let me know if the smoke bothers you. I'm happy to do what I can to minimize it." You don't have to promise that you'll never smoke (or grow) in the yard or on the balcony, but you can usually find compromises and reasonable solutions. Always respect H.O.A. or building rules.

Delivery Services

Delivery services can be really important, especially for patients who are in pain or can't drive to dispensaries or for those wanting to be discreet. Laws vary, so don't expect that each delivery service operates like the next—especially among counties and definitely among states. Like other service people in your life, there's an etiquette to your interactions with your cannabis delivery person, and it will depend heavily on the style of the delivery service. You may be asked for your ID at the time of the delivery to ensure you're twenty-one or over. As always, for the purposes of this book, we are only referring to *legal* engagement with cannabis delivery.

HOME DELIVERY VS. LOCATION DELIVERY

Depending on state law, you may be able to get your cannabis delivered to locations other than your home. Most delivery services practice discreet delivery: their company cars are not labeled, the delivery people don't wear uniforms, and some go so far as to have unidentifiable packaging.

As with many services today, technology can make cannabis delivery service easy: sometimes you can even track your driver, which can help with any timing or meet-up issues. You don't have to apologize for out-of-the-way locations, odd building instructions, or a fifth-floor walkup, but you should make such issues clear when placing the order via phone or in the notes section of your online order. Also be sure to indicate whether you prefer to have the delivery person come to the door or if you'd like to meet them down at the car. Always thank your delivery person for any extra efforts they may have made.

DURING THE DELIVERY

The classic conundrum of whether or not to hang with your delivery person is less of an issue with legal commercial delivery. Here are some things to consider.

Chitchat

This depends on the type of service you've engaged and where it's being delivered. If it's a drop-off service to your office, speed is usually the name of the game. A quick "Hey, how's your day going?" and a "Thank you" are all the chitchat the exchange needs. However, if you've chosen a company like California Wellness, which encourages their drivers to be educated enough to answer questions about product and offer demos, you might end up getting to know your delivery person well. If that relationship does develop, from time to time, you may have to navigate whether or not there's time for chitchat.

Things to Avoid

Don't invite drivers in to smoke or have a drink. They are at work and likely have other deliveries to make, and they often can't partake while on the clock. This goes for asking them to play video games or come in for a meal or get involved in roommate or relationship dramas as well.

Check Your Order

Always double-check your order. The last thing you want is some gorgeous green and no papers to roll it with. Or even worse, to have gotten someone else's order.

Tipping

Depending on the service's practice and state law, there may be a delivery charge, but those don't always go to the drivers. When you place your first order, ask what the tipping policy is. If you're unsure, asking the delivery person is okay, too. "May I ask if you accept tips?" is the easiest and most direct way to get your answer. Because you're asking to ask, you aren't saying, "Do you want a tip?" which feels more crass and less like a thank-you. In terms of how much to tip, food delivery is generally a good model, where you're giving about $5 or 10 to 20 percent of the bill. For a quick drop-off, a $5 tip is appropriate. For a more involved or time-consuming delivery, a 10 to 20 percent tip is more fitting.

As with all regular service providers, you should consider your regular delivery person during your holiday thank-yous. Many people use the end of the year as a time to thank the service providers in their lives, and your neighborhood cannabis delivery person is definitely in the mix of people to consider. A thoughtful gift or an extra tip (usually the cost of your average delivery) is kind. Don't be surprised if your delivery service includes a thank-you to you at the holidays. Cannabis companies love giving back to the people who support them.

HIGHER ETIQUETTE TIP:
SEND FLOWER . . . AND MORE

Cannabis deliveries are a wonderful gift! Send prerolls to a dinner party you couldn't attend or a nug to cheer up a friend after a tough day. Unlike cut flowers, which are used during emotional moments and can be tied to gender stereotypes, sending cannabis can be done by anyone in almost any 420-friendly relationship, and it would be considered rad. Just don't send cannabis to someone's home or office if you aren't 100 percent sure they would welcome it.

ETIQUETTE FOR SESSIONS

CHAPTER 5

Puff-puff-pass indeed!

The dispensary workers, growers, entrepreneurs, and friends that I talked to in my research for this book all spoke about how much they love sharing cannabis with the people in their lives. For some, they have friends whom they only socialize with around pot. For others, it varies by circumstance. Getting high together and going for a hike or a walk, cooking and eating together, playing sports, crafting, and playing or listening to music are all common get-togethers that can include cannabis. The level of connection you can feel by having consumed cannabis with someone can be a special experience in life. Like everything, a little forethought and some good etiquette can make the experience exceptional—even if you're just straight chillin'.

Now, let's remember here we're talking about getting high with a little help from our friends. It's super unlikely that someone is going to get seriously ticked off if a bowl gets kicked (is finished) before it gets to them or if it gets passed the "wrong" way. For one thing, you're all getting high and not likely to get too bent out of shape (a nice side effect). For another, when herb is legal, it's not a big deal if you miss out—there's plenty around, and it's easy to get. That's a real game changer from the days of prohibition, when people would watch the joint get smaller and smaller and worry whether it would even make it to them when they had thrown down on the session.

Higher etiquette explores what session etiquette is like now in a legalized culture, where we pay homage both to the traditions of the old and embrace the freedom and variety of the new.

The Basics of Any Session

A session can be everyone consuming the same cannabis the same way, or it can be to each his own while hanging out together. Sessions won't always have a clear host and guest relationship to lean on for social cues. In general, when you are sessioning with folks, you want to be aware of the product, the equipment, and the other people present.

Inclusion is always a thoughtful place to start from when it comes to any session. While "safety meetings" (aka sessions) during prohibition could sometimes necessitate privacy, depending on who was around and how much herb you had, you might have kept your sesh on the down low. Others were usually respectful of a group going off on their own for a sesh and would only come if invited. With legalized cannabis, this isn't as much of an issue. But, if you're craving a private conversation over some green and want a private session, make sure it's really the right time and place for it.

Awareness around those who aren't participating is key. There are some polite considerations to make toward those who aren't consuming.

Check for comfort. If there's no clear host and you're combusting, it's polite to ask those who aren't consuming before sparking anything. "Is everybody cool with me lighting this?" you might say, holding up a blunt. However, "Would anyone prefer we take this outside?" is even more considerate, since it shows from the start your willingness to take the session outside or to a spot where secondhand smoke won't bother others. "That would be great. Thanks for asking!" is an easy reply from someone who would indeed appreciate not sitting in a room with secondhand smoke.

Offer a person cannabis once. If they decline, let them know that you are happy to have them ask for a hit or help themselves if they change their mind later on. Many folks find it annoying if friends ask them multiple times throughout a session if they'd like to hit the bong, joint, or rig. Trust that your friend really is "all good," and that they will speak up if they'd like to jump in.

Watch the smoke. Be especially aware of where smoke is drifting and where you are exhaling vape and smoke. Opening windows and turning on fans are excellent courtesies to extend; however, pay attention to the direction of airflow; you might be exacerbating the situation rather than fixing it.

In any session, there are two key cannabis etiquette guidelines that anyone in the session should follow:

1. **Ask first.** You are always in good stead when you ask a friend first before using their product or equipment, or your own in someone else's space. On a walk with a friend, you may not think you need to ask if lighting a joint is okay, but the gesture will be appreciated, especially if you're sharing it and it's the only one you've got on you. Your friend might want to save it until you get to your destination or are farther along on the walk. In someone's home, asking before touching or using someone else's equipment is important for both safety and comfort levels—this is especially true with dab rigs and glass. It's also okay to ask about product so that you know what you're consuming.

2. **Follow instructions.** This is easier said than done, depending on the type of cannabis you're consuming and how it hits you. Follow the instructions of whoever is serving you product or giving you their equipment to use. Following their instructions is a courtesy that shows respect and prevents awkward moments. Not following someone's instructions can ruin product, equipment, and the good time you're hoping to have together.

Getting Started

The who and how of starting a session is important to good cannabis etiquette.

FRESH HITS

One of the most universally known points of etiquette among those who smoke socially is ensuring that everyone has a fresh hit of green bud (meaning that each person to whom a bowl is passed will be touching flame to green flower as opposed to already burned bud). The flavor that you get from a fresh hit is superior, and this act of consideration is about ensuring everyone gets tasty tokes.

Green, freshies, fresh green, curb it, corner it, and nip it are all phrases related to a fresh hit of cannabis. To curb, corner, or nip: touch the flame to the edge of the bowl so that it does not engage the entire bowl surface but just a "corner" of the bowl. This leaves fresh green for others.

A gentle reminder of "Save me some green" can be appropriate if needed. But the reality is that most folks can just pack a new bowl or offer friends personal bowls to resolve any issues about not having tasted fresh green.

FIRST HITS

When it comes to starting a shared joint, bowl, or vape bag, who gets the first hit is mildly debated. Many folks subscribe to the idea that the roller should always hit the joint first but that the person packing a bowl should hand it to someone else to start. On the joint front, the idea is that the roller knows how they roll and how to get their joint (or blunt or spliff) going so that it doesn't "canoe" or "run," making for wasted weed and awkward ashing.

For smoking bowls, the idea that the person packing should offer it first to someone else seems to stem more from a spirit of taking care of your friends. These two observations being made, you'll see people who pack bowls and light them, and you'll find joint rollers who always hand it off for someone else to spark. What you rarely encounter is someone who shows their frustration if it doesn't go as they expected.

Sometimes, you might choose to offer the first hit or a personal bowl, snap, or rip to the honoree or host of a gathering, but for regular sessions, usually the person packing or rolling is the one who decides to whom the first hit goes.

Mixing and Matching

One of the first things that get established in a session—and usually without much effort—is whose product is going to be used for what when. Now, this varies depending on a few things, such as hosting style, and when, where, how, and with whom you are burning. However, it's important to note that some folks will throw down and offer to mix whatever cannabis they have together. (Mixing cannabis is also sometimes called a salad.) Others will match, meaning they'll pack this bowl or roll this J, and then the other person will pack or roll the next. Matching can also be used to mean that you're throwing down the same amount of herb in order to mix.

So what do you do when someone throws down or mixes product you don't want to smoke or use? Options range from declining with or without a reason to making a counteroffer with something else. "Hey, I brought some **Mt. Hood Magic**." "Oh, I've been loving this **9 Pound Hammer** for hanging out lately." Either you'll both realize you want to smoke different weed and choose personals, or one of you will pick up that the other is more intent on a particular strain.

Rotation Etiquette

The etiquette of session rotation focuses more on the direction of passing and whose turn it is, whereas passing etiquette is more about the timing of when you hand off to someone else.

At large parties and functions, it's not uncommon for cannabis to be free from the standard smoking circle and to flow freely to and from whoever would like it. But in smaller groups, circular rotation is still common. Rotation, of course, can depend on what type of consumption is happening. Will Hyde of Leafly.com described for me one of the big differences he noticed when dabbing hit the scene: "When you light up a joint, a circle forms, and when you pull out a rig, a line will form."

Whether you're up next in line at the rig or in a group of folks passing something around, you'll want to pay attention to rotation. It happens almost without thinking, but it's good to check when starting to hand someone the bowl or blunt. The offer of "here" as you hold out the item acts as a quick check that the person (a) still wants it, and (b) that it's their turn.

Stoners, regular users, and enthusiasts all will usually speak up and say, "Oh no, it goes to Miles next" if it was indeed meant to go to Miles next. Does it *really* matter if Miles is fourth to hit the blunt each time it goes around? No. But it's an act of consideration with regard to sharing that is well established and consistently used, even if it happens very naturally and casually.

When a bowl, joint, or pen is kicked and another is going to be immediately shared, it's polite to offer the first hit to the person who hit it before it was declared kicked. While the person who didn't get a hit is certainly a high priority, keep in mind that the person before her may have gotten a pretty beat hit, and offering to start the bowl with *that* person is a considerate thing to do.

JUMPING IN

With pot being more prevalent now, jumping in on a session isn't seen as much as the annoying display of opportunism as it once was. (Unless you really don't want to be hanging out with the person who has jumped into the session. But that's a different story.) When you're hanging out at home, this might take the form of a roommate who conveniently appears when something is sparked. The mooch could be harmless and well received, even encouraged, or completely annoying given a variety of factors. If you're the one passing by the living room when a sesh starts up, good etiquette would be to read the room before asking, "Hey, can I grab a hit?"

If it seems as if folks are in deep conversation or having their own hang, don't sit in. Instead, take a hit and bow out. If you're getting "the more the merrier" treatment from your roommate or the group, by all means join in. At larger functions, it's very common to have someone pop into a session for a hit and then pop out. "Let me get a hit off that" usually does mean just that, a hit (unless the hit is like seven hits at once—we all know that dude).

For those who don't want to enjoy all of the hits off a blunt that they might get during a friendly session, popping in and out of rotation a couple of times is fairly common. You might start by taking a rip on the first round, holding off for a couple of passes, and then taking a toke again before it's finished. You should feel confident in letting your friends know when you'd like to tap back in. "Can I get another hit?" is all it takes.

Passing

In general, passing etiquette is very similar to what we learned both at the dinner table and in the kindergarten circle: pass in one direction (either left or right), don't skip anyone (unless they have declined), and don't forget to keep passing (also called "bogarting," see page 95). It's not a big deal if someone forgets to pass or passes in the wrong direction (though it may mean some gentle teasing from friends). With the right

friends, the teasing can be fun and lighthearted. But avoid accusatory language, especially if you're consuming with new acquaintances. Lean toward, "Can I grab a hit off that?" While grammatically incorrect, it's a more relaxed approach than, "Dude, you gonna pass that joint or what?" (For more on passing etiquette, see Passing on page 94.)

When something is passed to you, you should feel confident asking whether anyone knows the strain of the item being passed. It's not a buzzkill; instead, it's right in line with conscientious consumption. If you'd rather skip it, you can then either pass the item on to someone else or let the person you declined it from do so.

Declining

While there will always be people who will always take a toke, most cannabis users are happy to decline cannabis and do so regularly. As regulation forces the industry to disclose more information about the flower and products that we use, individuals can become more particular about their consumption and therefore more comfortable declining the types of cannabis they don't want to consume. Now that cannabis is consumed openly, people are more likely taking care of their own consumption throughout the day and may not be as ready to join a session, whether it's hanging out with friends or attending a product meeting.

Just like declining an invitation, declining cannabis requires little or no explanation. The most common and easily accepted ways to decline: "I'm good, thanks" and "I'm all set, thank you though." You might choose to give more information especially in a situation where someone is eager to have you try their bud or product: "Thank you so much, but right now I need to pass." You can add: "... but I'd love to try it a little later (or take some to try at home)" if that fits your circumstance.

It's also polite to take a "no thank you" toke, if you are so inclined, to simply try something your host is offering. Many people (even industry folks like cannabis expert Will Hyde) often use this tiny toke at large events, where there is a lot of consumption and product tasting. In such cases, folks may not want to dab a giant dab, but they'll take a "no thank you" toke to taste the flavor and be considerate to the people they're meeting. To do so, either take a very small or short hit, or take a tasting hit, where you hold the smoke or vape in your mouth to get a taste and blow it out again. ("I swear I didn't inhale!")

So Gross

When it comes to enjoying pot with others, unless everyone turns to personals, you're going to end up dealing with sharing mouthpieces and joint/blunt/spliff ends all the time. It has the potential to get gross, and one of etiquette's main goals is to help you not gross out others. Two big concerns around most methods of sharing are germs and spit. Sometimes you care; sometimes you don't. Just because you kiss your spouse doesn't mean you want to put your mouth on a spit-laden bowl. And lips that are too wet on a joint end can ruin it (especially if it's crutch-/filter-less).

GERMS

As a matter of public health, it's a good idea not to share cannabis if you're sick. It's also a good idea to get into the habit of doing what you can to pass along a pipe that's as germ-free as possible. Using flame to sanitize the mouthpiece of a glass pipe or bong is one of the easiest ways to "de-germ" it before passing it on to someone, whereas wiping off the piece can help with spit but won't do much for germs. If you are concerned about germs, the default is to roll or pack personals or use your personal vape pen. If you're concerned that you might be contagious, bring your own method of use and let folks know you'll be rocking personals while you hang out so that you don't get anyone sick. (Or, you know, stay home and get better!)

SPIT

It baffles me how this one happens, but spit does happen when sharing pens, pipes, vaporizer whips and bags, and hookah mouthpieces. If you have a particularly wet whistle, it's considerate to get better about double-checking a mouthpiece before you pass it to someone else. A quick wipe or burn with a lighter takes care of it. As someone being handed a slobbery mouthpiece, don't make a big deal about it, but do discreetly wipe off the mouthpiece so that you don't have to use it in a less than ideal condition. Note that the proper hand placement for holding a chillum can actually help eliminate the issue of slobber and works for a variety of methods.

Breaking Things

Breaking glass or other equipment can be heart wrenching. Many people get attached to their pieces, and whether it's your first one that somehow goes flying through the air, hitting the corner of the counter just right and shattering into colorful shards, or the dab rig that your friend accidentally knocks onto your tile floor, breaking equipment is awful. Friends feel horrible, you feel horrible, and then there's the question of replacement.

Just like with your china, stemware, and linens, you only really want to put out what you can handle ruining while hosting. If a piece really is precious to you, only bring it out to share with friends when you feel really confident about those who are around. Many dabbers especially will only let certain friends handle their rigs; for everyone else, the owner sets up and serves.

If something does go wrong, the person who broke it should do their best to help rectify the situation. First, apologize. Yes. Of course it was an accident, but apologies are important and easy so they are always the first step toward fixing a mistake. Next, always offer to help clean up, taking cues from the owner regarding whether you are saving pieces in the hope of fixing something or replacing a smaller part or if it's vacuum and trash-bin city. Take your cues from the owner on attitude as well. When someone is mad because they have just lost something they love, that's not the time to be overly casual. Validate your friend's feelings. Don't add to the mix by asking for forgiveness over and over or by not letting it go.

Offering to pay for the item's repair or replacement if you can is kind. Few people will expect that you replace a thousand-dollar glass piece, but offering to contribute what you can is one of the kindest and most respectful things you can do to help repair the item and the relationship. If your friend refuses your offer, it's truly okay to let it go and accept that the apology and the offer to help replace the item were enough. Don't be surprised, however, if your friend does take you up on your offer. (This is why you only offer what you truly can commit to and feel good about.)

If it was your piece that was broken, try to keep your emotions in check and operate from a place of understanding that this was an accident. Little jabs or catty remarks of disappointment won't help the situation. It's okay to be mad, but don't let it ruin the rest of the sesh (even if the session ended because of the break).

The Last Hit

Last hit is only truly the last hit when there's no more cannabis to consume. That being said, everyone has their idea of when they will tap out. Christian Preston of Magnolia Road Cannabis Company suggests that when it comes to joints and spliffs, you may want to stop before you burn it to the bottom because the cannabis flower that's being combusted at the end of your J isn't fresh herb but rather herb that's had all the smoke and resin from the rest of the bone dragged through it. If you are using a paper crutch or filter, the heat from the cherry (which extends farther than the red burning cherry itself) is reaching the paper faster than the cherry will, so you are starting to burn paper even when your cherry is still a quarter to a half inch above your filter. All told, it's always best to ask first before assuming the doobie or bowl is finished: "It's getting down to the end. Do you still want it?"

Ending a Session

The time has come to say good-bye, and parting well is good etiquette. It's never fun when it's time to go, but saying good-bye is a simple courtesy worth the effort. It's best to avoid flat-out ghosting at all costs. You could really trip your friend out.

It's also good to avoid peace-ing out right after you all consume. Unless you admit that you must literally dab and dash when you're invited to sesh, you should make an effort to stay through a whole round and chill a minute. (Depending on how you consume, this may be a shorter or longer commitment to good etiquette.)

Do say good-bye to your friends and thank them for the session, the spirit, and the experience.

Or just stand up, give a wave and say, "Thanks, bud. Catchya later."

THE QUIRKS OF GETTING HIGH

When it comes to getting high together, there are definitely some common quirks—and corresponding points of etiquette—to be aware of. The degree to which these affect your social interactions will be a strong influencer in when, how, and with whom you choose to get high.

ONE-HIT WONDERS Whether it's an invigorating strain or one that knocks you out, one-hit wonders feel heavy effects from just one or two hits of cannabis. This only becomes problematic when you're meant to hang out with your friend, and instead, you end up napping on their couch. A sweet apology and (maybe some CBD to lighten the load in the future) is the polite move after waking.

———

THE PASSAGE OF TIME Minutes can feel like hours when you're high. And it's very common to comment on this while you're high.

———

DUDE, I'M SO HIGH There's talking about how high you are because you are just amazed by it and then there's talking about the kind of high you're experiencing. Both are mind-blowingly awesome for the person experiencing it but less awesome for those who are hearing it if it gets repeated over and over again.

———

MUNCHIE MACHINE Flavors, textures, and, of course, cannabinoids and terpenes that stimulate the senses can cause this munchie-zombie–like state. Be aware of going robotic and mindlessly munching away.

LIT UP Some strains of cannabis are going to make you a Chatty Cathy. The euphoria can be incredibly fun and stimulating, and true laughing fits can ensue, but it can also go overboard. Have fun, be light and bright, but keep it cool, man.

————

THE PHILOSOPHER One of the best reasons to consume cannabis is the deep and meaningful conversations that you can connect over when you've consumed. While this can be amazing, read the room. It might not be the moment for a deep dive into your perception of your own existence.

————

FORGETTING THINGS You're not likely to forget your kids or where you are, but during a conversation, it's very easy to lose . . . to lose your . . . what's it called? You know, there's like a specific phrase . . . train! TRAIN OF THOUGHT! Be patient with those who are having the classic "stoner moment" (which isn't limited only to words but can also be like forgetting to start the movie you were set to watch).

————

PERMA-GRIN Oh happy day indeed! It's great feeling like you can't stop smiling. Get ready for some sore cheeks!

SHALL WE GET HIGH?

CHAPTER 6

Yes, let's!

Far beyond joints and bongs, there are all kinds of manipulations you can do to any method of cannabis consumption to change the mechanics and the experience of getting high with your friends. For each form of consumption, there comes a standard operating procedure, courtesies to be mindful of, and problems to look out for. On top of that, not everyone operates the same way. So grab your pipe, hit your rig, roll it up, slap on a patch, drop a tincture, fill your pen, or pop a gummy. Let's explore the different ways you can consume cannabis, so you can keep it cool when things get fun . . . and funky!

Consuming cannabis breaks down into three main methods: inhaling it, ingesting it, and absorbing it. While inhaling is the most common method for a sesh, sessioning with edibles is real and different from infused or paired meals (which is why you'll find those in the entertaining section on page 126), and, believe it or not, there are some etiquette points to consider when sharing topicals with friends.

Smoking

Poking smot . . . er, smoking pot is the quintessential way to enjoy getting high. Smoking cannabis has instant results and is an easy way to share. The biggest etiquette concerns are around the smoke itself. Regardless of how much you might like the smell or feel that it dissipates quickly, secondhand smoke is just that—secondhand smoke. It may have different chemical properties from secondhand cigarette smoke, but it's still secondhand smoke, and it's important to be aware that not everyone is going to enjoy the smoke or being around it.

Rotation or passing, fresh green and first hits, handling with care, and last hits are our other major etiquette concerns. Clogging or ruining the product and bogarting (not passing while not hitting what's lit) can be some of the biggest etiquette faux pas one can make. (But remember, you're probably getting high with your friends, and they'll likely laugh off minor offenses.)

PIPES

Pipes (spoons, chillums, oneies, bowls, steamrollers) are a cannabis classic. They can be made of glass, wood, ceramic, metal, or fruits and vegetables. Pipes are used to consume dried and cured cannabis flower and usually consist of a chamber (bowl) to put your weed into and a hole at the mouthpiece to draw the air through the lit herb, into the pipe, and then to you. It's pretty simple. Some pipes have a carb, a hole that you cover (with your finger or thumb) while you build (draw, pull) the hit, and then you uncover it to allow airflow and actually inhale the hit. When it comes to smoking from pipes, there are a few notable points of etiquette to keep in mind.

Personals Some folks are always eager to pack up a personal bowl for friends to enjoy, and then they will pack their own. It's a different type of sharing, and it's best to establish that that's what you are offering someone from the get-go. When you decide to sesh, say something like, "Here, let me pack you a personal." That's your friend's tip-off that he can chill with it and not pass it 'til it kicks.

Sparking it People differ on who should actually spark the bowl. Some subscribe to the idea that if it's my weed and my bowl, I am the host—even if we aren't in my house—and I will offer it to you first as a courtesy. This stems from a nature of generosity within cannabis culture and the true pleasure of providing. Others will just light it up out of habit or because the friendships and the social aspect of it are so casual and familiar. Don't sweat it too much in either case.

Fresh green If a passed bowl is intended for more than one person, cornering the bowl is a common and established courtesy. (For more on how to properly corner a bowl, see Fresh Hits on page 76.) Lawn mowing (burning the whole surface of the packed bowl) is not appreciated by most tokers. Rarely will someone seriously call out the offender, but it's still an obnoxious and noticed breach of higher etiquette.

Discarding To discard a kicked bowl, people usually turn the bowl upside down, whack it into the palm of their hand, and find the nearest garbage to discard the burned weed. Less messy is to use a pokey to dig the burned bud out of the bowl and put it into an ashtray or indicated receptacle. If it's your home, remember to empty the ashtray regularly, and if you're a visitor, always ask where to discard. A note about the pokey: make sure the tool you pick up is okay to use. If you're hosting this hang or packing bowls for people, offer to discard the bowl for them as well. Think of it like clearing the table for the next course.

BONGS & BUBBLERS

Bongs and bubblers (water pipes, bings, billies, moofs, gravity bongs) are a wonderful step up from the basic pipe. They have water chambers that filter the smoke through the water as you take the hit. Contrary to the big hits and big coughs portrayed in pot pop culture, these chambers actually function to cool the smoke down and give it a smoother feel. The water also acts as an extra filtration system, catching any physical ash or plant matter that might have gotten caught up in the airflow of your hit. Bubblers (water pipes) offer the simple convenience of a pipe but with the added benefit of the water chamber. You simply fill the chamber, pack your bowl, and away you go! Bongs range in size and shape from tiny little 6-inch bongs to 4-foot intricate blown-glass behemoths.

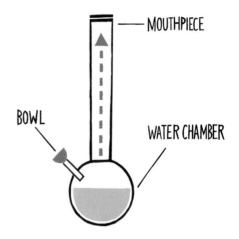

When it comes to smoking from water pipes, there are some etiquette highlights to keep in mind.

Clearing This is when you've gotten all the smoke out of the rising tube of a bong. Leaving the smoke there for more than a few moments will cause it to go stale. It's very common for folks to either offer for someone else to clear the bong or to just let the unhit smoke dissipate on its own.

Passing Bongs can be passed with a burning bowl, but for the most part, people pack a full snap (a personal hit/bowl all for you) for their friend to enjoy. And once it's cleared, the bong is repacked for a new person to hit. Remember, if a bong is being passed and not just meant as a snap, you'll want to corner the bowl for others to get some fresh green.

Big hits It's easy—especially with large bongs—to take too big a rip and cough. If you feel you've done this, immediately put the bong down or hand it off. The last thing anyone wants is a coughing fit that results in spilled bong water or, worse yet, a broken bong. And of course, don't cough into the bong—there will be bong water everywhere!

Spilling water This is just plain nasty. Bong or bubbler water is gross by anyone's standards, and spilling it usually results in a lingering undesirable aroma. Immediately help soak up the spilled water. Depending on where the water was spilled, you may want to try using the same organic cleaning agent you use to clean your piece. It's likely made of compounds that eat away at the resin in the bong water, giving you a better shot at truly cleaning the spill and eliminating the smell. If the water was spilled on a nice tablecloth or throw blanket, it's kind to offer to have it cleaned or to contribute to having it cleaned if that fits within your budget. (See Breaking Things on page 83.)

Keeping it clean Dirty glass affects the taste and experience of smoking weed so much that many folks will tell close friends without hesitation that a piece needs to be cleaned before they'll use it. Telling someone their piece isn't clean enough is a delicate issue, but stoners seem to blow by it easily among close friends. Depending on the situation, you may say something like, "Let's clean it first" or "Where's your cleaning solution? I'm happy to clean this before we use it" or "Dude, clean your bong. It's nasty." Think about your friend and the other people present so that you don't embarrass anyone, but for the most part you're in fine stead offering (or asking them) to clean their piece before a session.

JOINTS & SPLIFFS

Passing a good joint (J, jibber, doobie, bone, cone, fatty, bat, pinner) or a spliff is something many enthusiasts who have given up combustion still think of with fondness and appreciation. Easy to walk with, easy to chill with, and if rolled right, there's no need to relight, making the sharing of flower simple and familiar. A nice feature of the J is it requires no equipment to be used, and you can even buy it prerolled. Joints are made by taking finely broken-up dried and cured bud and rolling it in a smoking paper. Many joint rollers will either add a crutch or filter to make holding and smoking the joint or spliff easier. You can enhance joints many ways by adding kief and concentrate creatively.

Spliffs are joints with tobacco added to them and are very common in Europe. Tobacco can help a joint burn evenly and smoothly, although a well-rolled joint sans tobacco will also do the same thing. The tobacco provides nicotine, which adds a different type of boost to your high. Folks have furthered the distinctions down to a spliggerette, which is a spliff that is heavy on tobacco, and a sploint, a spliff heavier on the cannabis. Joints vary in size, shape, paper, rolling style, and smokeability, but no matter the jibber, the etiquette is usually the same.

Sparking While it's usually assumed to be a roller's choice when it comes to sparking doobies, it's best not to assume that your friends feel the same way. Show that you have some higher etiquette skills and ask folks who threw down herb on the joint if they'd like the first hit: "Do either of you want to spark it?" If they don't, fire away or offer it to the host or someone else. Anyone who is offered may accept or decline, as they wish. The roller may also spark it.

Passing Not all joint and spliff smokers pass after the same number of puffs. Some folks will encourage you to chill with it awhile and to pass it once you're finished. Others will want to keep it moving and will stick to the traditional puff-puff-pass. If you're smoking with someone for the first time and you want to fit in, it's never bad form to ask about passing. A simple "Puff-puff-pass or do y'all chill with it?" will easily get you a response you can work with. Different tokes for different folks. And if you know that you tend to forget to pass, it's never bad to invite people to remind you. "I smoke personals a lot. Please give me a heads-up if I'm holding on to this."

Rotation "Paaaaaaasss the dutchie on the left-hand side . . ." (thank you, Musical Youth) is good advice . . . most of the time. While typically pot is passed to the left (I'm 99 percent convinced this is due solely to that song), rotation doesn't always happen in a nice little circle. At many gatherings, joints may be passed randomly, or you may even have a few different strains being passed at once. The takeaway is to pay attention to the general rotation style at a gathering and follow that lead. You can always look to your host or to the person who brought or sparked the joint to see what they did, or you can ask, "Which way is this going?" or "Who'd like this next?" (Speak up if you want it next.)

Don't bogart Bogarting is a term derived from the way Humphrey Bogart would just let a cigarette hang out of his mouth, not seeming to actually smoke it. Bogarting a joint is when you are holding on to it or wasting it by letting it burn down without being hit. Another phrase that's commonly heard is, "It's not a microphone." Translation: you're wasting weed I want. If you're talking and you're not smoking the joint or passing it, don't be surprised if someone calls you on it.

Ashing Use any ashtray that is provided. Try not to flick a joint or blunt hard when ashing; instead, tap the ash off into the ashtray.

No pinching Try not to pinch the joint, which will cause the resinated cannabis to smush together, decrease airflow, and make the joint harder to smoke. If the joint has a crutch or filter, always try to hold it and pass it in a way that allows the next person to take hold of the filter as well. There is nothing more annoying than rolling with a crutch and having someone pinch the flower portion of the joint. Don't do that.

Canoes and runs Rolled items will occasionally "canoe" or "run," burning down one side faster than the other. To fix it, wet your finger (water is more polite; spit works in a pinch) and apply it to the lower side, helping to slow the paper from burning while the other side catches up, or you can burn it off entirely. (See image on page 130.) Caught early, it's no big deal, but if left, a run can ruin a joint by making the cherry huge. Don't draw heavily on a canoeing joint; this can make it worse.

Clogged joint If a doobie has clogged up with resin, you may be able to pull the filter (if there is one) out a little ways to create a bit more airflow. If the filter is where the resin is collecting, you can pull it out, cut off the resinated end, and reinsert it. But, depending on where the clog is happening, you may want to cut off the cherry and resinated end and either reroll what you can or pack it into a bowl. Or you can ditch it and just roll a new joint with fresh herb.

Holes and tears You can easily fix holes and tears either by using your finger to lightly cover the hole while you take a hit or by using a small patch from your paper's gum. Just tear or cut off a little square, lightly wet either the patch or the area you want it to cover, and Band-Aid your joint right up. Give it a sec to dry and continue enjoying.

The last hit Before just declaring a spliff or a joint finished, ask the group. First, you offer it to the next person in rotation. If they are all set, you can then offer it to the person after them or to the group and see if there are any takers. Many folks bail out on joints and spliffs as they get down to the last ¼ inch, but others will burn it down to the end. An easy ask to the group will ensure that no one is pining for lost weed. If no one wants it, you're clear to take that last hit. If you don't want it, stub it out.

KIEF-ING IT REAL

Kief (see page 28) ends up on everything that the flower touches: hands, scissors, jars, and, of course, grinders. Do be aware of someone's built-up kief either in a jar or a grinder. If you open someone else's grinder to use it and see a bunch of built-up kief along the edges or coating the bottom, DO NOT DISCARD IT! It's kind to ask whether the person is saving it or whether you should deposit it somewhere before just dumping it into the blunt or bowl. If it's okay for you to use it, ask if there's a way they prefer to scrape it out. Some folks have a sensitivity around plastic or glass being scraped in order to get the kief, the worry being that small bits of plastic or glass will get into the kief. Asking first is the thoughtful thing to do.

BLUNTS

Blunts (L, dutch, dutchie, philly, cannon, bluntski, B, Bleezy/Bleez-e) get their own special section because blunts are different from joints and spliffs. Rolled using the emptied-out tobacco leaves that wrap a cigar, blunts are a big deal. The tobacco leaf wrapper (which you can also buy as a blunt wrap) adds a whole other tobacco-cannabis combo beyond the spliff. Blunts hit hard, meaning the high is intensified by the tobacco, and you'll feel that combination. Crack it, dump it, fill it, roll it, lick it (a lot), light it, hit it.

While blunt courtesy follows most of the same basic principles as joints and spliffs (though you wouldn't put a filter or crutch in a blunt), there are some cannon-specific courtesies to consider.

Flavors Flavoring seems to find its way into all kinds of spaces when it comes to cannabis, and flavored blunt wraps are no exception. If you have picked up a flavored wrap, be sure to check with those you'll be smoking it with to make sure they're down. And if you're bringing a flavored blunt to share, it's kind to let folks know ahead of time, since many have preferences—be it of the actual flavor or whether they even inhale flavored products.

Clean rolling Blunt rolling can get messy when you dump the tobacco from the cigar. Before you roll, be sure you're set up to keep things clean (roll over a smooth surface and have a receptacle nearby). Cleaning up before you spark it is kind, too.

Lighting it As with joints, it's typically the roller's choice unless there's an honoree for the session (see First Hits on page 77).

Puffs and passing Blunt smokers usually hit an L three times as opposed to the standard two hits off a joint.

Pinching This is a little different than with joints and spliffs. How well you can pinch the blunt as you get down to the end of it will greatly determine how much you can get out of it. Those who are dexterous will be able to hang 'til the end. Unless someone has a roach clip (or something similar, like tweezers or needlenose pliers), it can get hard to hold the end of a blunt to hit it.

The last hit This is very similar to joint or spliff etiquette—keep passing until the person next to you declines, and if they do, you can offer it up to the group before finishing it off or stubbing it out.

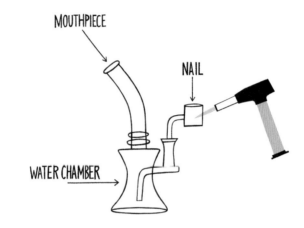

MOUTHPIECE

NAIL

WATER CHAMBER

Dabbing

Dabbing consists of taking cannabis concentrate (a dab) and dropping (dabbing) it onto a heated element (nail or banger). The rest of the rig and process is much like using a bubbler: the smoke/vapor is collected in the glass chamber of the rig, and as you draw air through the rig, the vapor passes through the water (cooling it down) and then to you. This gives you a clean, flavorful hit like no other. (Note: Rigs can have domed or domeless nails.)

The precision of dabbing is exquisite. With temperature control and products that are tailor-made for specific terpene-cannabinoid combinations, dabbing is the luxury automobile of cannabis consumption: elegant and powerful. At first glance, many are turned off by the clear pipe, blowtorch, and one-hit wonder of it all. But taking a closer look, low-temp dabbing with electric nails has little resemblance to anything illicit and offers all the elegance the cannabis community has craved.

A low-temp dab connoisseur will pair product and temperature perfectly to ignite the senses with taste, aroma, and, of course, the wonderfully smooth texture of vapor. Now there's low-temp dabbing and then there's dabbing. Many dabbers dab at high temperatures, even when they allow their nails to cool before dabbing a dab. Some people want the cloudy, bonglike experience (not always present in low-temp dabbing).

Temperature guides on sites like Leafly.com and from companies like Goldleaf (shopgoldleaf.com) offer information on temperature control and how it affects your high and the product you're consuming. (See page 35 for activation temperatures for specific compounds.) Lower temperatures (220° to 400°F) preserve terpenes (flavor) and give lighter highs that are often more focused and functional. Higher temperatures (400° to 500°F) produce a heavier high, with more intense euphoria and a very relaxed, meditative, or drowsy effect. Beyond 500°F, you lose a lot of the benefits and flavors from the cannabinoids and terpenes. You're still going to enjoy your cannabis and feel effects, but you won't be getting its maximum entourage effect potential.

Regardless of heat levels, don't let the intricacies of the dab rig or the intensity of the possible blowtorch scare you off. Instead, embrace the accoutrement like a chef embraces the excitement of the *enflambé*! (Or, heat the banger, dab the dab, rip it, and enjoy.)

Since dab rigs can be expensive and tricky to operate, it's important to be extracourteous when using someone else's rig. If you are the owner, it's appropriate to let your friends know the ins and outs of how you like others to use your rig. Here are some things to keep in mind.

IF IT'S YOUR RIG . . .

It's kind for rig owners to communicate clearly what is being offered to the people who are dabbing with them. Some rig owners will want to use their concentrate and work the rig for you; others are happy to have you use your own concentrate, but they will prepare the dab. Still others are fine with your taking care of both the concentrate and the dab on your own. Clear communication from the get-go helps, such as saying,

"Here, let me get a dab going for ya. Here's what I have for concentrate." Or, "Hey, if you want to dab, feel free; the rig and the dabs are right there. Just ask me if you need anything."

Most rig owners don't want other people working their rigs unless they know the person well. Burnt bangers and the desire for the owner to be mad at herself and not others if anything breaks are the big drivers for this protectiveness.

Cleaning up A clean nail means a clean hit. Use a cotton swab or a small piece of paper towel to clean a warm nail head after the hit so the next hit is fresh.

Pacing As a dabber, it's polite to be mindful of newbies and help them to not overdo it. A dab the size of half a grain of rice is a good starting point. When you take a dab for the first time and it's smooth and easy and you're getting all that terpene goodness, it's easy to want to take another and another. Help guide your newbie friend to a good experience by suggesting you pace your session and keep your dabs on the smaller side to start.

IF IT'S NOT YOUR RIG . . .

It's respectful to ask before touching someone else's rig—some of these rigs can run into the hundreds and even thousands of dollars. Many rigs are set up in a specific location in a home, and the dab will be taken there. It's fine to request using your personal mouthpiece if you carry one with you. It's also fine to offer to use your own extract or concentrate, but if the rig owner says they'd prefer that their own product be used, be prepared to run with that or decline. If you're allowed to dab for yourself and it's not an electric nail, ask about nail-cooling times. Different rigs, torches, and product can all account for your host suggesting a specific time or heat to aim for when dropping a dab. The goal is to avoid chazzing the banger, which is when you take a dab that is too hot and scorch the banger (nail). This can ruin the quality and physical appearance of the banger/nail. It can also mean you're using the product at too high a temperature, which can affect the taste and quality of the dab.

Guest cleanup Offer to clean the nail head after your hit so that the next person is presented with a fresh, clean banger. Your host may do it anyway, but it's kind to make the offer.

Vaping

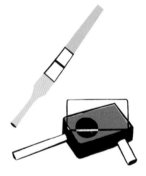

It was thought that the invention of the vape pen would obliterate session etiquette altogether, since pens make it possible for people to easily take care of themselves. But I'm happy to report that nearly a decade in, we're still sharing vape sessions—and loving it. In order to really be vaping, you aren't burning the product but rather converting a solid to a gas. Some vapor can look like cloudy smoke, either by happenstance or on purpose. It can also have a slight aroma.

Vaporizers come in many forms and can be powered by batteries or power outlets. Vape pens, which can be refillable or disposable, are a convenient option for many. While most use oil cartridges or other concentrates, some are designed for flower, and others work with both. You can even add a water apparatus to your vape pen, which allows for a second layer of filtration and a smoother hit. Portable vaporizers require no outlets and are also great for individual use. They are not the easiest to share, though, since they don't hold charges well and there is sometimes a learning curve for how to hit them. There are also tabletop vaporizers, which aren't as portable but are a ton of fun. Some use a bag with a closeable mouthpiece to collect the vapor that you then take the hit from. Others use a long plastic whip with a mouthpiece on one end and a bowl on the other. Tabletop devices, once meant only for flower, now have attachments for concentrates.

Those who are looking to lighten the load on their lungs, taste more, or who want a more discreet consumption experience often seek vapor. Low-temperature vaporizing also allows for a better terpene-cannabinoid experience because you aren't burning the terpenes beyond their boiling points, and you are achieving maximum flavor. For those seeking the health benefits of cannabis vaporizing, it's imperative to make sure that your device is truly vaporizing and at the right temperature. (See activation temperatures on page 35.) There are many devices on the market labeled as vaporization devices, but they actually burn the product and some can even deliver more harmful substances into your system. Pay close attention to the equipment you own and use. Monitor its settings to ensure you're truly vaporizing.

Much of the common courtesy you practice when vaping will depend on what type of device you are using. Here are some things to keep in mind.

PENS AND PORTABLE VAPORIZERS

In states where cannabis is legalized, vape pens are less of a communal device and more of a personal one. But that doesn't stop people from asking or from feeling as if they should offer a hit from their pen or portable vaporizer. If you're going to share, offer a brief explanation of what product is in it and how to hit the device effectively. If you have an attachment for your device (which usually creates a water filter), it's kind to set the entire hit up so that the only thing your friend has to do is take a rip.

Concentrate reminder If you're vaping concentrate, it's kind to remind folks that this is a concentrate. One of the issues people have is that a vape pen is easy to hit like a joint, but it's waaay more potent. You may want to hit it all night long—oral fixation, something to do with your hands, it's fun—but that's a lot of cannabis, my friend, especially if you're not used to it. Take care with dosage when using concentrates.

Mouthpiece etiquette It's considerate to wipe the mouthpiece before handing it to someone. Or, if it's being handed to you, offer to use your own mouthpiece—many folks now carry a spare with them. Don't burn the mouthpiece with a lighter as you would a glass bowl, since these pieces are often made of plastic or silicone.

Repacking This needs to happen more often with flower vape pens and portable vaporizers because they can't hold that much weed in them. The owner of the device will usually repack it, or you can offer your own green.

Respecting Mother Earth It's considerate to ask if a disposable pen is recyclable and how to do so.

Overheating a vape pen If you hold a button too long or pull and pull on a vape pen, it can make the pen taste horrible for the rest of the cartridge. If it feels harsh or tastes like plastic, you've gone too far. Now you'll have to decide to stick with a burnt cartridge or start a new one. If you burn a cartridge that's not yours, apologize to the person and consider picking up a replacement the next time you're at the dispensary (or make a point to do so).

Dead batteries When your device has lost its charge and doesn't have enough power to be used, it's definitely a buzzkill . . . one that nonelectric-method users might feel inclined to tease a newfangled portable vape user for. Avoid the urge.

VAPE BAGS

The vape bags used with tabletop vaporizers can usually be made to fit any size group. Whether it's a big or small bag, take your hit and keep passing it. Unlike a joint that might self-extinguish if someone starts bogarting it, the vape bag will go stale. The vapor in it is fresh for only about 10 minutes or less. So take your hit and pass it on. If you're hosting and want someone to have a bag for themselves, let them know this from the start, and if you have size options, let them choose how big a bag to vape.

Giving guidance The owner of the device should always explain the product being used, the type of heat, and any settings or function information: "Press the button twice for a midtemp range" or "I'm preparing this whole bag for you."

Ingesting

Sessioning with edibles and drinkables is a time commitment and brings a different pace and vibe to your sesh. Instead of meeting up for a quick bowl, get yourself into the mental space of staying awhile. We're talking a four- to eight-hour hangout here. You want to session with people whose company you enjoy. While vape bags, doobies, and bowls focus on the event of consuming, sessioning with edibles brings to mind the entertaining vibes of sitting on a front porch, backyard stoop, or dock while the sun sets on a casual summer night. The biggest etiquette concern when it comes to ingestibles of any kind: communicate the type, potency, and dosage of what's available. Cannabis culture cares about being responsible, and communication is the first step.

Because ingesting cannabis brings the cannabinoids and terpenes into your system by metabolizing them through the liver, it's important to remember that your high won't take effect immediately, and it will be stronger than inhaling. (For more on ingesting, see The Physiology of Getting High on page 37.) For those who metabolize slowly, sessioning with edibles may not even be feasible, since the high may take effect when you're ready to finish the session or even long after the session. I cannot stress enough that when consuming edibles, give yourself a safety net—do not plan to go anywhere for a few hours (at least four to eight for maximum assurance). For some folks, 10mg is nothing; they won't even notice they've consumed cannabis. For others, it will knock them out all night—or at least for a few hours.

Because of the time-intensive nature of edibles and drinkables, there are certain courtesies to consider when sessioning with them. (For more information, see Infusions & Pairing Parties on page 126.)

EDIBLES

Cannabis-infused edibles come in so many forms, from the infused cannabis Rice Krispies squares your roommate makes to manufactured cannabis base ingredients (salt, sugars, powders, oils, butters, syrups, and so on) and premade infused foods of all kinds (gummies, chocolates, cookies, and granola, to name a few). Decarbing weed allows for it to be bioavailable, and you can add it to virtually anything. Using infused oils and other ingredients is highly popular, although it's sometimes more time-consuming to make. Here are some considerations to think about when sessioning with edibles.

Noncannabis food Offering noncannabis food when you're sessioning with edibles is a good idea. Often, when we take a bite of something, we want to take another bite. It's very easy with poppable pot to grab the nearest bowl of whatever, forgetting that the whatever may have an extra 10mg of cannabis per serving.

Labeling is key Whether you use the manufacturer's label or create a homemade label to accompany the manufacturer's label, state the type, potency, and dosage of the items you're offering. Providing more information is always better than less. Here are some examples: "macarons, about 5mg of African Queen per cookie"; "African Queen, 25 percent THC, ß-myrcene, and a-pinene dominant"; or "African Queen macarons: positive and relaxing head high."

Your edible spread It's not a bad idea to think of setting out your spread for the hangout by putting your cannabis edibles in one area (maybe even on a totally different table) away from your noncannabis food so that no one absentmindedly starts robo-munchie-ing the brownies.

Slumber parties Offer to host your friends for the night or at least until their edible highs wear off for certain. Making this offer as part of the invitation is higher etiquette.

DRINKABLES

From homemade tinctures to add to your favorite punches and cocktails to premade beverages like freshly squeezed canna-orange juice (part of a canna-complete breakfast!), there are many ways to infuse both alcoholic and nonalcoholic drinks with cannabis. (And no, you won't get the spins if you do this right.) The nice thing about making or buying infused beverages is that you can tailor the experience. With a joint, unless you decide to roll personals, you're smoking the same cannabis for that session (which is a great thing, if you all really like that strain). But with tinctures and infusions, you can share the drink but tailor the amount of cannabis by making your glass exactly as you'd like it to be, while still using the same mixer that your friend is drinking. Or vice versa: you can tailor the drink but share the same cannabis. It's also a nice way for cannabis consumers to enjoy a drink. Consider the following when deciding to session with drinkable cannabis.

Variety counts Whether you're purchasing premade infused drinks or you're mixing your own cannabis concoctions, the etiquette for drinkable sessions is much like the etiquette for having a friend over for a casual drink. You want to make sure you have some variety to offer and that you're informing your friend about her options. You might choose to have a couple of tinctures that vary in their potency and the cultivars they come from so that your friend can choose what she likes. Or your friend might bring over her favorite tincture and add it to whatever drink you're making together.

Deciding how much Whether your goal is to have one drink and be high or to try a few different concoctions, it's a good idea to decide this ahead of time so you can gauge the potency and dosage for your drinks.

Premade or homemade You'll also want to decide ahead of time (just as you would when cooking food) whether you're going to be making mixtures this time around—break out that juicer—or buying premade mixes or drinks. Either is perfectly acceptable.

Transportation As with any ingestible adventure, be sure that your friends have a place to crash if the high is lasting longer than anticipated. It's always better to err on the side of safety and take someone's keys if you have to.

Labeling glasses If there are more than two people drinking cannabis together, you'll want to find a way to label your glasses so that everyone knows whose is whose.

Not your usual bottle of Bud The proverbial bottle of wine as a host gift can be a cannabis go-to as well. Cannabis wines, beers, and infused liquors make excellent gifts. There are two rules to follow: the gift must be labeled very clearly, and you should know your host is comfortable mixing alcohol and cannabis.

Polite tasting Good session etiquette dictates that if you'd like to try someone else's drink, ask first and use a straw to taste. Take the straw (preferably reusable), dip it into the drink as far as you'd like, put your thumb or finger over the top end to hold the liquid in the straw, and then remove the straw from your friend's glass, holding it over your mouth and releasing your thumb or finger so the liquid releases.

Cheers! Literally. "Cheers-ing" as you start your session is a great way to practice higher etiquette.

Absorbing

Topicals, patches, and sublinguals are all transdermal ways of consuming cannabis. Some products can even double as ingestibles and topicals. Absorbing cannabis hasn't really caught on as a way to session with friends, but there are a couple of things to consider when applying some salve or passing a sublingual.

The biggest etiquette concerns with transdermals are about safety and comfort. You don't want friends or family accidentally putting on a salve or rub when they meant to use something nonmedicated. And when it comes to comfort, it's worth considering the time and place you're in before you ask someone to put salve on a hard-to-reach spot.

TOPICALS, SALVES & RUBS

Whether it's a massage train or a friend asking for a little rub to put on a specific ache, it's always polite to inform friends of the recommended amount for the dosage listed on the packaging (usually pea size to start). You'll also want to help maximize the effects. If a rub is better used after a hot shower—but you don't want to offer that to your friend—you could offer a warm washcloth to heat the skin instead.

Depending on where the aching body part is, it's also a great idea to offer your friend a private place to put on the rub. If you feel comfortable and the ache is in a hard-to-reach spot, you could also offer to help apply the salve. But usually it's best to say, "If you'd like . . ." "If it's easier . . .", or "If you're comfortable with it . . ." before the offer. Not all friends are okay with stripping down and slathering up.

And if you are the friend asking for the rub, definitely don't just whip your shirt off and present your back. First, say something like, "Do you have something that could help me apply this, or would you be willing to put it on my back?" By including the option of a tool that might help, you help limit the potential for this ask to sound like a precursor to some hanky-panky.

PATCHES

For patches, again, we're falling back to the two key cannabis etiquette points: ask first and follow instructions. Whether it's rereading the package or asking your friend to confirm, you want to make sure that any patch you put on is really the one you meant to put on. And remember, you can take a patch off anytime. It would definitely be poor etiquette to slap a patch on someone who didn't know you were doing so.

SUBLINGUALS

Sublinguals are liquid forms of cannabis, usually tinctures. They are meant to be taken by placing the liquid under your tongue. The cannabis is still getting into your system transdermally, but because of the nature of the lining in your mouth, it absorbs very quickly and activates in your system quickly, too.

Many people share droppers when taking sublinguals, and it's important to remember that you don't want to touch the dropper to your mouth.

In cannabis culture, people don't really get together by bringing a bunch of sublinguals to drop, but it's very possible that rather than adding the tincture to a beverage, you might simply take a drop under your tongue and pass the tincture along.

Ask first and follow the instructions of the person who brought the sublingual.

ENTERTAINING & CANNABIS

CHAPTER 7

Napkin, pipe, fork, knife, spoon, lighter . . .

Cannabis sessions can happen any time, but intentional cannabis entertaining is a whole different ball game. The goal for any host is to make guests feel comfortable in their home. In return, a guest's goal is to participate in their host's offerings and not to abuse a host's generosity or standards in their home.

It's worth taking the time to think about how cannabis is going to fit into your entertaining style. Some hosts might always have a cannabis option; others might have cannabis come and go from their social calendar, depending on the event and the guest list. The biggest considerations for hosts to keep in mind are to communicate the *type of function* being thrown as well as the *effect* and *potency* of any cannabis they provide.

Invitations

From the ultracasual "Wanna hang?" to a formal printed or handwritten dinner party invitation, when you live in a state where cannabis is legal (and especially where legalization is new), it's polite to let your guests know when inviting them whether or not this gathering is going to be a "pro" or "no" cannabis party. While preemptively letting folks know if it's okay to toke up at your party may seem like overkill, there are plenty of situations where you find yourself socializing with people you've just met or where you're in a mix of social groups. In these cases, it's nice to give a heads-up. To a friend who smokes pot regularly at your house, you might let him or her know if this particular gathering will be different from the usual house rules.

Few of us expect our hosts to say, "By the way, we serve alcohol at our house," but for folks who abstain, it's nice to get that information up front. It's the same thing regarding indoor cigarette use or fears or allergies around pets. It's kind when a host alerts a new guest to a few of the things to expect upon visiting their home. This is so much better than having your guests accept your invitation and then realize as you spark a joint during the cocktail hour, that they are uncomfortable and unsure of how to back out without offending you—or stay and compromise their own comfort levels. It would be nice not to worry about this, but since we are still in the early years of legalization, it's best to err on the side of higher etiquette: a good host lets guests know what to expect before the gathering.

A note about your guest list: while you may want to include all of your friends, for those folks who abstain from pot, being invited to a cannabis-heavy party is akin to not drinking bourbon and being invited to a bourbon tasting. The inclusion is appreciated; however, it's not their scene—they know it and that's okay.

A GOOD HOST COMMUNICATES

As the host, you set the standard in your own home, and it's up to you to make decisions and then communicate them clearly and kindly to your guests when you issue your invitation.

Host decides: I plan to provide pot and welcome guests to bring their own, either for personal use or to share.
Host communicates: "So glad you can come for dinner on Friday night. I have a bunch of good herb on hand but please feel free to bring whatever works for you if you'd like."

———

Host decides: Tonight is not a ganja gathering.
Host communicates: "Unlike other gatherings, this one will not be 420 friendly."

———

Host decides: BYOP, BYOC . . . Bring Your Own whatever you want to call it.
Host communicates: "Thursday, 6:00 to 9:00 p.m., heavy hors d'oeuvres, and BYOW (Bring Your Own Weed)."

———

Host decides: It's a pot potluck.
Host communicates: "Please bring your favorite side dish and a nug for the party!"

The Home Cannabis Bar

The home cannabis bar is a celebration of the themes of sharing and generosity that are at the heart of the cannabis community. The idea that you could offer your guests a number of different strains and ways to enjoy them is a cannabis dream come true. Your cannabis bar can be as simple or extravagant as you like. You might choose to have some basic equipment on hand or you may have a full-blown dispensary's worth of options for your guests.

STOCKING POT

How much and what type of cannabis you stock in your bar for entertaining will greatly depend on your preferences, your hosting style, and
your budget. For any of the following categories of product, gravitate
first toward what you would personally use and then consider what
would be good for your guests. At the least, you're ensuring that your
bar is stocked with items you're familiar with and can describe to your
guests. For each of the following products, consider keeping a couple of
different strains that are geared toward varying effects and, if you really
want to give your guests options, consider some different potencies as
well. Being able to offer your guests a range of options is helpful toward
everyone having a good time.

Flower Most folks have their everyday herb, their sharing herb, and their
superspecial herb. When considering your guests' preferences, try to
fill in the gaps rather than getting more of what you already have. Don't
forget to check when the flower you bought was harvested, since it starts
to degrade after a year. Kief is nice to keep on hand for guests who are
looking for something a little more potent to add to their bowl or joint.
And prerolls are a great hosting option since they are so darn convenient. Storage matters, too, for flower; jars and tins with humidity packs
or a Cannador (cannabis humidor) are great solutions for keeping your
herb fresh and ready for a good time.

Concentrates You might keep a variety of strains and cartridge types on
hand for vape pen users. Similarly, it's nice to keep options on hand for
dabs and vaping (such as budder/wax, shatter, rosin, live resin, oils, or
crumble). Much of your decision will be based on what you like using
with your rig. If you consider stocking tinctures for the home cannabis
bar, store them in a cool, dark place.

Salves and patches Topicals such as Rescue Rub, transdermal gel pens,
and a variety of patches are good to keep on hand. These can be great
options for those who may not want edibles or to inhale but would like
a cannabis experience.

HOW MANY GRAMS PER GUEST?

This really depends on your budget, your preferences, and how you're consuming. A quarter to a half gram of flower per guest per session throughout the night would be a good starting place. If you think you're going to send your bong around a few times throughout the night and you have eight guests think 0.2g x 8 guests x 3 sessions = 4.8g for the evening. Getting a little more is never a bad idea, you might not need a full quarter (7g) but 5g or 5.5g should be good. Up the amount for heavier consumers or go lighter when need be. (Note for concentrates you'll purchase far less but you can spend quite a lot quickly. Since different forms and different potencies will play a large roll in what you purchase, ask your local budtender for suggestions.)

If you're serving joints, a 0.7-gram joint (a large preroll) will be good for three to five people (or more if your friends are light consumers, or your pot is potent). Try to estimate one three- to five-person joint for every two to three hours if consuming throughout the night. You may need more or less depending on your guest's consumption habits or how you choose to incorporate cannabis into the evening. Joints tend to use more herb because they keep burning while folks talk, hold, and pass them. Factor this in when choosing doobies for your dinner party. You might choose to serve them just during the cocktail hour or after dessert. As a host, it's up to you to set the pace, so do what feels right with your hosting style, guest list and reason for gathering.

While it's nice for a host to try to balance her preferences for the party with her guests' needs, remember, too, that personal joints, bowls, and vape pens will allow guests to take hits in between a host's offerings.

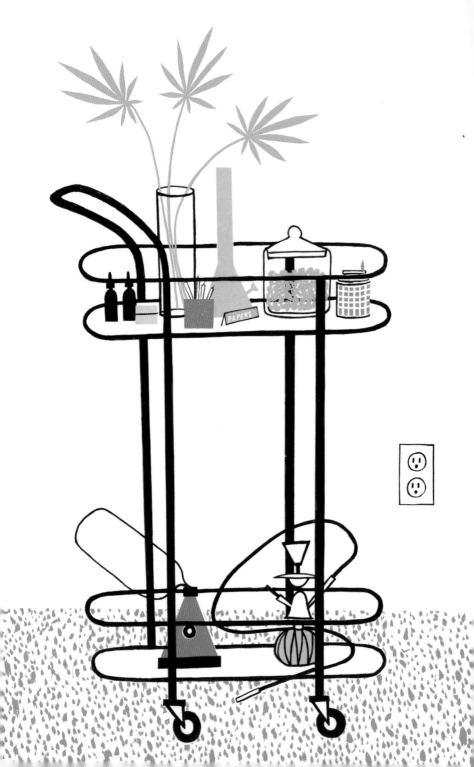

Edibles Having a selection of flavors and forms is always a good idea but do remember to keep an eye on expiration dates and potency, and for safety be sure to keep them in their original packaging when storing so that it's clear they are cannabis products.

Premade drinks These are a great addition to your canna-bar. While you can easily add tinctures to any beverage, sometimes it's fun to try a premade option. Don't forget cannabis wine, beer, and liquor as options.

YOUR EQUIPMENT

Just as you might select special glasses, shakers, ice molds, and other specialty equipment for your home cocktail bar, it's nice for the 420-friendly host to stock a range of equipment with which guests can enjoy cannabis. Be sure to keep your equipment clean and in good working order to maximize everyone's comfort and enjoyment.

Rolling materials Do stock a selection of rolling papers, blunts and blunt wraps, crutches/filters (try glass or ceramic for something classy and reusable), and a grinder (electric or manual) or a chop cup (a shot glass works well) and scissors.

Glass While one good spoon and a bong or bubbler will suffice, there is no limit to how much glass is too much glass to have on hand. (Mini-joint/blunt bubblers, anyone?)

Vaporizer A tabletop device can work for flower, concentrate, or both. If using a bag vaporizer, be sure to keep a good supply of bags or bag material on hand.

Vape pens and portable vaporizers From disposables to dual-capability high-tech pens, keeping some form of vape pen or portable vaporizer in your bar is a great idea.

Dab rig You might set up your dab rig in a specific place in your house, or it might be part of your bud bar. If you aren't using an electric nail, be sure to remember fuel for your blowtorch.

Fire Lighters and matches are the go-to choice but consider old-school table lighters. Usually heavy and elegant at the same time, these table fixtures mean you never lose your lighter (although you do have to refill these antiques). Hemp wick is also a great option for those wanting to stay away from the flavors and chemicals associated with lighters and matches.

Cleaning supplies While alcohol is a standard cannabis equipment cleaner, organic cleaning agents are a safer option because they eat away at the resins that cause the intense smell without creating fumes. If you do use alcohol to clean your equipment, be sure to air the equipment out for a bit before reusing. When cleaning spills, consider using an organic agent (test on a patch before applying to fabric, carpet, or upholstery). The agent will help take care of the odor. This is also a good idea when pouring dirty bong water down the drain. Adding a bit of cleaning solution to it can keep the room fresh while you sesh.

Hosting Your Ganja Guests

People celebrate with food and drink in many different ways. The same goes for cannabis—it can be a big part of the celebration or a casual component. But no matter which, as the host of a gathering, you'll want to be prepared to assist your guests in any way possible. Being able to tell your guests what you know about what you are offering them is key to their having a good time (and staying safe).

While we advise guests to stick with what they are offered by their host when it comes to food and drink, I have a hard time imagining a scenario where a host would be offended that a guest wants to hit their own vape pen instead of the household bong. If a guest wants to enjoy cannabis in a method other than what you've provided for your party, that's okay. You might even make them feel more comfortable by encouraging them. "Hey, Kate, I know you don't love smoking out of glass. Would you like me to roll up a joint for you instead?" Etiquette can be so easy.

In general, a good host gets to know their friends' preferences over time and, when possible, will accommodate them as part of the party planning, whether that's dialing things back for a guest who is less canna-comfortable or ensuring that guests who are enthusiasts have the strains and equipment they prefer to enjoy. An aware host always keeps his guests' comfort and enjoyment at the forefront of his actions.

With cannabis newbies, it's important to go low and slow and talk with them about where their comfort levels are. Encourage newbies to take it easy and absorb their experience before taking another dab, eating another edible, or puffing down a preroll.

HOSTS LEAD THE WAY

As the host, it's up to you to guide your guests through their time and experience at your gathering. It's so easy to think people will simply make themselves comfortable, and yet a host stepping up and leading the way is actually what makes guests feel encouraged to participate and enjoy the party.

- Guide your guest through any usage you need to assist with or explain. Not everyone knows how to hit a volcano or take a dab. Asking guests if they've used an apparatus before and offering to walk them through it is thoughtful and responsible.

- Pay attention to the finer points such as who a bowl kicked on, when a joint might need to be passed, or the rotation of a session. While anyone can call out a point of etiquette, it's nice to have a host paying attention and facilitating the flow if needed.

- Don't pressure folks who decline to take a hit. It's okay to check in a few hits later, but after that, it's kinder to let your guests know that they can speak up if they'd like to take a hit, but otherwise, you'll skip them in rotation.

- Be aware of whose weed is being used. It's kind to thank guests who are sharing weed at your gathering.

- At larger parties, let your guests know what they may help themselves to and where it's okay to enjoy weed.

- Setting out ashtrays and discard bowls is thoughtful, not only for keeping joint and blunt smoking clean and contained but also for discarding pipe and bong bowls as well.

CANNA-COURTESY

Offering a glass of water to your guests from the get-go is a good way to ensure that folks have had at least some water before consuming pot. With the natural tendency for cannabis to dehydrate, providing guests with easy access to water is not just considerate, it's also responsible.

MUNCHIE CONSIDERATIONS

As a host, preparing for the munchies is a true kindness to your guests. There is nothing worse than getting hit hard by a desire to satisfy every taste and texture you can think of when you're at someone else's home, and you don't want to be rude by raiding their kitchen or bolting to the nearest convenience store. Cannabis enhances the senses, so, hosts, consider offering a variety of textures and flavors when possible. Crunchy, smooth, and chewy can all satisfy a craving for a texture. A minibuffet of flavors is a pothead's dream—salty, sweet, savory, bitter, sour, umami—oh my!

RECEIVING A HOST GIFT

Your kind guests might bring you some kind bud as a hosting gift. While your first reaction should be an enthusiastic, "How thoughtful. Thank you!" it's all right for you to ask about the bud you've been given: "May I ask what strain it is?" or "What are the effects like?"

Much like the classic bottle of wine or box of chocolates, the question of whether it's intended to be enjoyed during the occasion is a bit of a dance between the guest and the host. The guest might say, "I rolled this up, not for tonight, but for you to enjoy as you wish." Or they might say, "I brought this as a contribution to tonight if you'd like it." While it's always a host's choice to spark something, in general, if a host knows the strain or if it isn't going to interfere with the plan for the evening, go ahead and enjoy that joint, nug, or concentrate at the party.

If a friend has brought you a host gift that is not something you feel comfortable consuming, consider graciously accepting it and either letting your guest know you will save it for another time or just simply not partake of it yourself. If you want to go a little further, it can be polite to positively comment on the bud's aroma or appearance or take a tasting toke to get the flavor without inhaling. No matter what you choose to do, appreciate and focus on the gesture of the gift.

OFFERING HOMEGROWN

Some hosts might offer their homegrown bud. When doing so, tell your guests what you know about your homegrown, such as the strain(s) and growing methods used. When you're in a state where regulation and testing provide reliable safety nets, consuming homegrown may be more of a concern to some simply because your guests are more familiar with having access to and trusting test results. Don't be offended if someone turns down your homegrown because they just aren't sure how it will hit them.

DANKSGIVING

A Danksgiving is a Thanksgiving-style meal among cannabis-loving friends that's usually held around Thanksgiving but could occur at any time of the year. At a Danksgiving, either much weed is smoked or the meal itself is infused with cannabis (or both!). The number-one rule with Danksgivings is safety. Each guest should make arrangements (if the host has not already offered) either for transportation at the end of the evening or for staying the night. Cannabis can have a much more potent effect when ingested, but even if you're combusting or vaping all night, it's still smart to make safe travel or sleeping arrangements.

If you're invited to a Danksgiving, it's considered polite to bring a dish and, or, some bud. If you're asked to bring an infused dish and haven't cooked with cannabis before, it's best to admit your knowledge level to your host. Maybe you and your host can cook something together so you can learn. If there isn't time for that, your host may ask you to bring something noninfused or suggest a refrigerated option from a local dispensary. You can often buy infused butter (not to be confused with budder) at a dispensary and then make something you already know how to bake. Or pick up something like an infused balsamic vinegar, honey, or chocolate. Do double-check about dosing and potency so you know what you are bringing to the party and can tell other guests.

Sending a handwritten thank-you note to your host afterward would be a higher etiquette move for sure.

Guest Etiquette

From bringing flower instead of flowers to having in-depth labels for the food you bring, as a cannabis-consuming guest, there are a few considerations to take into account, whether the gathering is heavily herb friendly or not. Cannabis may be legalized in your state, but that doesn't mean it's encouraged everywhere all the time. Most consumers do head out the door with something to take care of their personal needs as well as with something to share if the moment arises. A good guest will be prepared to positively roll with whatever situation they find themselves in.

RESPECT YOUR HOST'S REQUESTS

If your host asks that you "smoke outside," "not bring edibles into the house," "use the ashtrays rather than ashing on the patio," or whatever it is, it's important to respect the request. It's their home and while their goal is to make you comfortable, a host shouldn't be made to feel uncomfortable in their own home.

While many consumers will simply bring something with them to a party and read the room as to whether or not they will actually spark or use it, asking first is a smarter move if you're thinking of making a contribution and you're unsure of what kind of event it will be. Text your friend and ask: "Looking forward to tonight; happy to bring some bud to contribute to the party. Let me know!" If you know it will be a ganja-friendly gathering, it's also a classy move to bring cannabis to share *and* cannabis as a gift for your host. Just let your host know: "Suraya, I brought this to share tonight if you'd like, and I brought *this* for you and Maya as a gift." It should go without saying that you shouldn't bring your host schwag—your old, stale bud is not kind bud to gift. That being said, contributions of just about any kind are still seen as good higher etiquette.

Be aware that your host might have reasons for not taking you up on your party offering—just like a bottle of wine, it's up to the host to decide if the gift is used at the party or not. It isn't necessary to gift wrap nugget, prerolled joints, or other cannabis hosting gifts, although having something to present the cannabis in is usually preferable to just pulling it out of a sweaty shirt pocket or dirty purse corner. A KushKard (see page 132) is a great go-to, especially for joints, blunts, spliffs, cartridges, and disposable pens.

POT FOR PERSONAL USE

There are times when you are a guest and realize you don't know the host's preference for cannabis use. Before you just hit your pen, it's always best to ask. The key in this moment is to ask in a way that shows your host you are willing and able to take your cannabis elsewhere to enjoy it. "Do you mind if I vape in here, or would you prefer I go elsewhere?"

When the vibe at the party isn't "Feel free to spark that doobie," taking care of yourself becomes slightly more delicate. No matter what a bummer it might be not to toke freely, as a good guest, you'll want to be aware and respectful of your hosts and the other guests. Just as you wouldn't walk into a room and light a cigarette without asking, discreetly ask your host if there's a good place to vape or smoke for a minute. If you can tell that even just stepping outside wouldn't be the best idea, it means you're on your own for finding a place, or you'll have to wait. This is why it's good to have a few different consumption methods that work for you, especially methods that eliminate smoke or vapor.

Most cannabis users will admit to vaping in a bathroom if their host doesn't allow cannabis in their home. While this most certainly works and isn't likely to leave behind any odor, it is not higher etiquette. It's inconsiderate to your host and their choices about their home.

MIND YOUR MUNCHIES

While some folks don't get the munchies, others get them hard core. It's one of the funnier effects of getting high and a real asset to those with a loss of appetite. The trick is to make sure your munchies don't degrade your dining skills or infringe upon your host's generosity. It's so easy to get locked into a munchie-zombie–like state, but be mindful of your manners when the munchies strike. Remember to chew with your mouth closed, drink water, and be sure others have a chance to enjoy what's being offered . . . if you can. It's okay to ask a friend to keep you in check. All that warning aside, the munchies can be so much fun and bring a whole other level of enjoyment of sensations to your gathering.

RESPECTING THE HOMEGROWN

People are often really proud of their homegrown. Some folks have worked on strains for years and lovingly tend their plants. Others just grow what they can from whatever seeds or starters they get. As a guest, you want to be polite when it comes to your host's homegrown, whether he is showing you the living plants or offering you a hit, a nug, or homemade concentrate. Phrasing questions out of curiosity rather than skepticism is kind, as is keeping the focus on their grow and their plants rather than replying to each statement they make with how you grow yours. A conversation should be more than two people making statements about their own worlds. Reflect, ask questions, and find positive comments to share. This is a precious part of the sharing in the cannabis community.

IT'S EASY TO DECLINE

If you're not into the strain, type, or method being offered, a guest can say, "I'm all set, thanks!" or "I'm good for now but thank you." (For more on declining, see Etiquette for Sessions on page 81.)

CANNABIS PREFERENCES

If you have particular preferences about the product that you consume, then just as with a dietary restriction, it's okay to ask about a product you're being offered and then either partake or not, based on the response. "Do you know the strain?" "What kind of effects has it given you?" If you get an answer that doesn't align with what you want to consume, you can say, "Thanks for letting me know. I'm good for now but thank you." The goal is to get the information you need without making the other person feel judged.

Infusions & Pairing Parties

Infusions (where cannabis has been fully incorporated into the food) and paired meals (where a strain of flower or concentrate is matched with food and drink) offer an array of dining experiences to embrace. When it comes to whether or not your next dinner should be infused or paired, most canna-pros like Ry Prichard of Viceland's *Bong Appétit* advise you to do both by serving both infused and noninfused dishes. It's important to make people feel comfortable, and not everyone may be onboard with eating cannabis all evening. It's best to have an array of noninfused dishes on hand so that guests can have a whole meal without cannabis (not just one dish) but still smoke/vape something.

INFUSED DISHES & MEALS

The complex flavors that can emerge when you infuse foods with cannabis are extraordinary. Despite the known potency of ingesting cannabis, you can create entire edible meals that won't burn out your guests. The trick is to keep the potency of all the infused dishes low so that if guests aren't exercising moderation, they still won't get baked to oblivion. The etiquette of an infused meal is much the same as the etiquette of a noninfused meal. Enjoy the food, monitor your intake and participate in the conversation.

Macarons
AFRICAN QUEEN
23% THC
RELAXED, HAPPY HIGH

In preparing an edible meal, you might choose to focus on low-temperature infused oils to season your food. This allows terpenes to be the main star of the dish. They aren't heated to high enough temperatures to engage the full potency of the THC. Adding tincture to items is also an easy way to make an edible that you can gauge the dosage of more easily. The hardest thing with homemade edibles is that even trusted recipes can test at different levels. Pretesting by creating make-ahead dishes that reheat nicely as well as using low doses so that folks can eat more than one item are good ways to help your guests enjoy an edible evening at your home.

Everything infused should be clearly labeled with any relevant information: the strain, potency, cannabinoids, terpenes, likely effects, your personal experience. It's also a good idea to keep the noninfused dishes totally separate to reduce the risk of unintentional consumption. And, of course, no edible should be where pets or someone who is underage could access it. For mixed-age parties, many 420 hosts will even set up a separate area with a clearly defined border or boundary where products and consumption are contained, with a designated "watchdog" keeping an eye on the area.

PAIRED DINNERS

A paired dinner alters the timing and table setting of a meal because you are smoking or vaping cannabis at the table in order to enhance the flavor and experience of the meal as well as just to enjoy cannabis at the dinner table. Guests may be encouraged to rotate through puffing, eating, and drinking at the meal, or cannabis smoke or vapor may be served between courses. The host should lead the way.

Part of the fun of preparing for a paired meal is searching for strains and aromas to pair with the meal. But don't forget to pay attention to the potency of the pot you're pairing. You don't want to end up pairing your entire meal with 27 percent THC strains when your guests aren't heavy hitters.

It's a good idea to use the flavor descriptions of different terpenes to determine what strains and terpenes to highlight or pair in your meal. Once you know the flavor notes of different terpenes, you'll be able to mix and match them with flavors you know and love for a unique and exploratory experience with your guests. You can always test your pairings out ahead of time to ensure you have good combinations for the actual meal.

Ry Prichard suggests that one good place to start is with Lemon Kush Butter an amazing addition to fish, asparagus, artichokes, and more. (Talk about elevating a recipe!)

Table Setting for a Paired Meal

There are many ways to creatively add cannabis accoutrements to your table setting for a paired meal. Philip Wolf of Cultivating Spirits, a company specializing in paired and infused cannabis dining experiences, suggests the following for a meal paired with flower smoked out of glass pipes: place the pipe to the left of the setting with a dish of cannabis above the pipe; place the diner's lighter and hemp wick (if being used) to the right of the setting.

Hemp wick (or a vegan version) is a great option at a tasting meal, since it does not impact the flavor of the hit as much as inhaling off flame from a lighter or a match. The setting described reflects a right hand–dominant diner. The diner holds the pipe in her left hand, uses the right hand to pick up the flower from the dish and pack the bowl, and then uses her right hand to pick up the lighter and spark the bowl.

Other Consumption Options

Like the standard table setting, at a paired meal, you want items logically placed so that diners can move through the experience with ease. While bowls are a bit easier to do pairings with at the table, many other consumption options can also work just fine.

You might consider serving one or two joints (depending on the size) for an eight-person table so that the joint makes it through two to four rotations and everyone gets a taste of it. You could consider serving personals, but that's a lot of combustion at the table unless you're giving out pinner-sized personals (teeny tiny thin joints). Serving joints is also a wonderful way to close out dinner at the end of the meal—a joint served after dessert with coffee or tea would be lovely. Here are some other items to consider when serving guests at the table.

Vape pens These may be used at the table, and if so, they may be placed to the right of the setting or across the top of the setting either between the place card and dessertware or behind the place card. Just make sure the pen is visible to the diner when he or she is seated.

Ashtrays Although Emily Post may have cringed when it came to having cigarettes at the table prior to coffee, if you're pairing cannabis flower during a meal, giving diners a place to ash or discard is key to cleanliness and comfort at the table. Place a pokey for cleaning out bowls with the ashtray, and it will indicate that it's okay to use the ashtray to discard the bowl. Alternatively, you could give each diner their own ashtray if doing so won't clutter the table.

Candles A traditional table setting element, candles serve a tempting functionality to combustors. Don't pick up a candlestick (or lean over one) to light your bowl or joint. (Gasp!) Do pay attention to whether the candles are being provided to light hemp wick at the table. A good host will clearly provide a lighter or matches if the candles are not meant to be used, but in their absence, ask first before lighting your hemp wick from the dining table candles.

The host could also bring out dab rigs, bongs, bubblers, or tabletop vaping devices to accompany the meal. As the host, you want to make sure that whatever the apparatus, you have room for it at the table.

HIGHER ETIQUETTE TIPS

Who cleans up? A host should empty the ashtrays at the table as each course is cleared—or sooner if need be.

To each their own. While hosts shouldn't feel they have to go out of their way, being able to provide personal smoking devices for each diner at the meal is preferable to passing items that everyone will put their mouth on while eating.

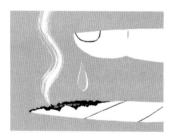

Anticipate troubleshooting. If you are serving joints throughout the meal or at the end of the meal, consider putting out a finger bowl so that if a joint canoes or runs, you (or a guest) can use a finger dipped in clean water to fix the run, rather than putting spit on your finger or using your tongue at the table.

Drinkables

Whether it's canna-cocktails, beverages infused with cannabis, or tinctures in mixers, the cocktail party is getting a revamp from legalized cannabis culture. Books such as Warren Bobrow's *Cannabis Cocktails, Mocktails & Tonics* offer an array of recipes and ideas for how to safely infuse liquids with cannabis. Whether you're including alcohol or not, offering guests "buzz-worthy libations" is a fun way to enjoy cannabis in the familiar setting of a cocktail party. Pairing terpene-strong tinctures with fruit juices, spices, syrups, tonics, and quality sparkling or spring water can be the focus of the evening with guests having fun keeping track of their favorites. Or you might choose to make a couple of pitchers of cannabis concoctions and have some signature drinks to try for the evening.

As with every cannabis offering, be sure to give as much information as you can about the cannabis you used in your beverages, its potency, and what the potential effects might be so that guests can make educated choices throughout the evening. Bobrow advises that you always start off your guests with a glass of water to help them hydrate and to keep water available throughout the party, while also encouraging that it be consumed to help counteract any adverse effects.

If a guest ever feels uncomfortably high, you can provide them with either a decent dose of CBD (25mg or more) or a mixture that Bobrow recommends of freshly squeezed juice from six organic lemons and a few peppercorns to counteract the feeling. You can add seltzer and honey to the mixture to make it more palatable.

Gifts with Lift

When considering bringing a cannabis gift to your host, you have a
range of options for both the items and their presentation. A great time
to gift to your cannabis buddies is on birthdays and holidays, especially
cannabis holidays: the classic 420 on April 20 and the emerging 710
on July 10, which honors the dabbing and concentrates community.
Remember, too, you don't have to consume a certain type of cannabis
or consume at all to give it as a gift. The gift itself isn't about your own
interest as much as it is about the person receiving it.

CANNABIS CARDS

KushKards and other similar brands are specifically designed to be able
to hold joints and other cannabis items, and some even include a match
and match strike. While these cards can't be sent through the mail
with the cannabis in them, they are a wonderful way to present a joint,
cannabis lollipop, blunt, spliff, oil cartridge, or disposable vape pen.
Remember to write on the card the strain of the product or how potent it
is. If you want to send a card to a friend in the mail, you can always add
a rolled-up $10 or $20 bill and say, "The next blunt's on me."

DO WE SMOKE IT TOGETHER?

If you've gifted someone cannabis in a usable form and you give it to
them in person, they may choose whether to enjoy it with you or not.
Typically the person receiving it will share it with the giver, but that's
not always the case, so it's best not to assume that it will be sparked
right away. If your intent is to partake of the item you're presenting to a
friend, then just share a session with them. But if you truly want to gift,
you can't have expectations about that joint being smoked with you. As
the giver, it's classy to have something else to consume together for your
hangout and really let the gift remain a gift for the person receiving it.

HOST GIFT SUGGESTIONS

Not sure what to give your kind host (or the doja lover in your life)? Here are some suggestions to help you select just the right ganja gift:

- Any type of cannabis product, homegrown, flower, or concentrate that you think your host might enjoy
- Nice rolling papers or reusable crutches/filters
- A selection of joints, either prerolls or rolled by you
- Salves and rubs
- Dugouts, both artisan and novelty (golf ball stash jar and golf tee pipe anyone?)
- Small pipes
- Nug jars
- Edibles
- Homemade or store-bought infusions or tinctures
- Stylish cannabis labels to use for parties (think cheese-board signs)

CANNABIS ABOUT TOWN

CHAPTER 8

Oh, the places you'll go!
Oh, the weed that you'll see!

The American entrepreneurial spirit thrives as legalized cannabis grows. Cannabis-linked businesses are sprouting up in surprising places and ways, providing the average person with a number of options regarding how to engage and socialize with cannabis.

The tourism industry brings us canna-bus tours, grow tours, 420-friendly hotels, and other adventures to explore. The food and beverage industry is booming with infused and paired dining experiences, chefs are cooking for medicinal patients, and the world of edible products is ever expanding. There are cannabis yoga classes, creative classes (puff 'n' paint), growing groups, educational events, social clubs, product parties, party parties (high teas), and B2B (business-to-business) events.

Companies like Oregrown have sophisticated style that doesn't put pot in the consumer's face yet still celebrates it. And there is an entire cannabis health and beauty product industry. The list of cannadventures, opportunities, and products is endless. Here is just a brief sampling of how you may choose to engage with cannabis about town and the best ways to go about it.

The Dispensary

A store that you can go into that has a variety of herb available really is a dank dream come true. The novelty alone is what draws some people to engage, where before legalization, they would not have. But not all dispensaries are the same. In selecting a dispensary, it's a smart idea to read reviews online and look for shops that respect customers' preferences and take the time to explain products. Dispensaries that only talk about potency or type of bud, despite being sources for good weed, may not provide the educational experience a newbie or patient might need. And even experienced users can benefit from going to shops where the staff really knows their stuff, since they can be great places to find out about new products and brands.

BEFORE YOU GO

In order to enter a dispensary, you must have a valid photo ID (with expiration and birth date) and in some cases it's cash only for payment. In some states, foreign visitors also need their passports to purchase pot.

Some states let you bring devices or products into the store, while others do not. If you have a question about a broken pen or other item, call first and ask how the dispensary would like to handle it.

In most dispensaries, dogs and anyone under the age of twenty-one cannot enter with you. In many places, you can bring a baby into a restaurant and have a drink, but you cannot bring a baby into a dispensary (even though consumption is not allowed onsite).

AT THE DISPENSARY

When you go through the door of a dispensary, you will often find yourself in an entrance or waiting area (though not always; you may be able to walk right in). This is the check-in point, where you'll present your ID before going into the dispensary. There are capacity limits at dispensaries, so you may have to take a seat in a waiting area before being escorted into the store, or you may be allowed right in. If a dispensary is busy, you may have a bit of a wait, especially during high-traffic times (the lunch hour and between 5:00 and 7:00 p.m.). Laws and regulations are continuously changing, and budtenders and dispensaries have to comply in order to stay open. Be patient if the procedure at your favorite shop changes. Some dispensaries are still cash-only businesses, but you'll usually find an ATM in the waiting area. If you make a purchase, you'll likely need to present your ID multiple times during your visit, so it's not a bad idea to keep your ID handy and be patient with the dispensary's procedures.

People who work at dispensaries are noted for their excellent customer service, professionalism, and welcoming attitudes. Usually the same person (a budtender or educator) will work with you throughout your visit, provide you with as much information as you'd like, and encourage you to spend time with them to make sure you feel good about the products you're purchasing. You should always feel free to ask questions and let your budtender or even the person at check-in know if it's your first time at that dispensary. Budtenders are incredibly knowledgeable and can advise you on the effects you're seeking and the best products to get them from. Or you can ask your budtender's opinion about the products they enjoy.

Budtenders will let you know how much you can interact with the cannabis flower. Some stores love letting you pick up the big jars of flower and stick your face in to breathe the aromas; others won't let you touch the jars, but budtenders may hold them out for you to sniff. Sometimes, the product is completely prepackaged. Nowhere do they let you touch the bud.

WHAT *NOT* TO DO AT A DISPENSARY

While dispensary rules may vary, these six points are good to keep in mind:

1. **Don't talk about taking anything out of state**. If you mention planes, luggage, or the shipping of cannabis or equipment in any form, your budtender may have to ask you to leave.

2. **Avoid picking up the big glass jars of buds**. There's often hundreds of dollars' worth of weed in one jar, and if you drop it, the broken glass makes the product unsafe. It's pretty much the biggest faux pas you can make. That being said, some dispensaries allow it; the easy solution is to ask first.

3. **Don't touch the flower**. Hands have germs and oils on them, and the pressure on the nuggets themselves can be described as "wear and tear." None of this is good for the product or for the people purchasing it. Most dispensaries have tongs to handle the actual flower.

4. **Refrain from getting upset if a strain is out of stock or listed at a certain price**. There are websites you can use (like weedmaps.com) to get up-to-date stock info on the current cost of the strains you love. If you're seeking something specific, it's a good idea to call the dispensary before you go. Some popular strains run out within hours of being stocked.

5. **Don't insult the bud**. Most dispensaries are proud of their growers, and if you don't have something nice to say, it's best to avoid saying anything at all. You can always say, "I'm hearing you, but I'm not drawn to it" if a budtender recommends something you're not interested in.

6. **. . . or budtender opinions**. If you ask a budtender their opinion, please know that (a) it's only an opinion, and (b) it's not polite to then tell the budtender they are wrong about their opinion.

420-Friendly Facilities

As more states legalize recreational and adult use and as communities get more comfortable with cannabis establishments, the ability to find 420-friendly facilities is getting—and will continue to get—easier. Usually a 420-friendly facility will make its pot policy clear; some even market their ability to allow consumption on-site. But if you're unsure, ask, "Are you a cannabis-friendly facility?" If you get the go-ahead, it's important to respect the rules set forth by the establishment, whether it's using a designated smoking area or only vaping indoors. Not doing so could get you fined or kicked out.

ETIQUETTE FOR PUBLIC CONSUMPTION

Here are some considerations to take when choosing an open public place to puff:

- Who else is around?
- What direction is the wind blowing?
- Is there anywhere else to go?
- Remember to be a good ambassador. If someone is bothered by combustion, rather than get defensive, roll with it. Politely finding another place where the smoke won't affect them shows your understanding and consideration.
- Dispose of any roaches or disposable pens appropriately.

BUD 'N' BREAKFASTS

A bud 'n' breakfast is simply a cannabis-friendly bed and breakfast. If you book a room, you'll be sent or told about specific guidelines regarding consumption in your room, in the common areas of the facility, and on the grounds.

Most B&Bs can't sell you cannabis, but there might be a house stash the proprietor invites you to use. However, it's best not to rely solely on the house stash. Some B&Bs have partnerships with local dispensaries that will deliver or take special care of B&B guests sent by the proprietor.

Common Spaces

If you'd like to consume in a common space, it's kind to ask first before sparking your joint or bowl or hitting your vape. Guests have no obligation to share their cannabis with one another or with the proprietor. However, more often than not, if guests are consuming in a common area, they will make the offer. Some guests make plans to consume together.

Cleanliness & Consideration

Most bud 'n' breakfasts do their best to give guests everything they need to considerately consume cannabis. Ashtrays with a discard tool to help clean out your bowl may be placed in each room and around the common areas. They sometimes offer a glass library so that you don't have to purchase while you travel. If your B&B has provided a blowie or a smoke bottle (used to exhale smoke into so it makes less of an impact indoors), it's definitely considerate to use it, since it reduces the amount of smoke that seeps into the walls and linens in a room.

Tobacco Use

Most bud 'n' breakfasts are strict about no-tobacco usage in the house. This means spliffs and blunts are out of the question and those who typically mix a bowl with tobacco need to refrain when consuming inside at the B&B.

Saying Thank You

Many guests will leave the proprietor any leftover product as a tip or a thank you, or they may offer to contribute it to the house stash. While giving bud is always kind, leaving a cash tip is still a thoughtful gesture for housekeeping. Remember to say thank you for your stay.

Cannactivities

There are all kinds of cannabis activities and classes you can sign up for, from social clubs that throw parties and host events to product awareness gatherings, creative consumption events, health classes, and lectures. Whether it's a hobby or a social or special interest group, there's a way to do the things you love and connect over cannabis, too.

Depending on local and state laws, you may be meeting at an event space or in a private home. You may be encouraged to bring cannabis with you, or, depending on the event and the laws of the particular location, you may be offered different types of products by the organization, instructor, or host. Be sure to double-check the invitation or posting for information about what to bring and what will be provided.

This is one of those times when it's a good idea to bring some extra to share. While you will not be expected to share, hosts usually make it clear that you should feel welcome to offer other attendees what you have. Like most cannabis-sharing etiquette, it's always kind to offer what information you know about your product. If someone hasn't told you what they have, it's perfectly fine to ask, "Ooh, thank you. May I ask what you've got?"

THINGS TO BE AWARE OF

While the events you attend will vary, the following are some common considerations.

Location & Event Space

Many cannactivities take place at private residences due to consumption laws. You may not see a location on the posting or invitation; instead, you may see a neighborhood or area listed so that you can roughly gauge travel. If there is no information listed, you can email the hosts to ask the area or neighborhood where the event will be held. If you are visiting a stranger's home, keep an eye out for indicators on the posting of what door to enter, access codes to use, and where to park. Once you're at the event, your host and the instructor will let you know which parts of the house are available for the event. It's not in the spirit of higher etiquette to go snooping around someone's home or enter rooms you haven't been invited to.

Punctuality & Gratitude

No different from noncannabis classes and events, punctuality is important. Some classes won't admit you after a certain point, and others will start without you. It's best to buffer your travel time so that you can be punctual. After the class, it's considerate to say thank you to the other attendees, the hosts, and the instructor to honor the time and experience you've shared together. Don't linger too long; your host or instructor will likely have to move on with their day.

Positive Participation

Whether it's a health class, costume party, creative writing group, or cooking experience, participating positively and respectfully is extremely important. It's polite to be upbeat and to go with the vibe the event is trying to create because it respects and honors the safe space created by the hosts and instructors. Bring your supportive, encouraging vibes to the class.

A Good Attendee . . .

- Pays attention to instructions and respects that others have also come to share in this experience.

- Respects others' level of participation or experience, both with cannabis and the topic of the gathering.

- Is accountable for his or her own body and makes instructors aware of any quirks or potential side effects that he or she may experience.

- Offers to be helpful during class and respects the space and items being used.

- Is enthusiastic yet patient with other participants and with the hosts and instructors.

- Expresses his or her appreciation for the group, the space, and the shared experience.

HEALTH CLASSES

Yoga and other health and well-being practices offer cannabis classes where you can consume cannabis before or during the class to enhance the practice. Many find this beneficial for both mind and body. Here is a place where paying attention to how a strain will affect you and any quirks you may experience on it is imperative to enjoying the class.

CREATIVE CLASSES

Whether it's a "lit on lit," "smoke and stitch," or a "puff 'n' paint" class, cannabis is a wonderful aid for the creative mind. With specific strains being developed to foster motivation and creativity, combining the open, social aspects of writing groups, art classes, and other creative mediums with cannabis is a great way to be social and get inspired.

It's important to read the room during creative cannabis classes. Depending on the nature of the class and its participants, some folks may tap into emotional spaces, so you want to take care with your responses. These classes aren't meant solely as group critiques, and while some people might welcome feedback, the place to start is with encouragement.

PARTY PARTIES

Social membership groups, product parties, B2B parties, events hosted by your favorite dispensary—there are a lot of cannabis parties to attend that don't require an invitation from a friend. Pay attention to the party description so that you know if there are instructions for arrival, anything you need to bring, or a dress code you need to adhere to or aim for. As always, it's polite to arrive on time.

When you enter the event, it will be clear either from displays or stations at the party what you can consume and where. Alternatively, greeters may welcome you and let you know what can be consumed when and where—even if that comes in the form of "Please, help yourself at any time."

These parties can run the gamut when it comes to formality. Paired and infused sit-down dinner parties could be a jeans and T-shirt affair or a semiformal affair. Some events play up the whimsical and fantasy elements of consuming cannabis, and others bring a sophisticated, intellectual, or elegant vibe. Pay attention to the invitation for clues about the formality and vibe of the event.

Like all parties and events, it's also important to self-regulate when consuming and be smart about your transportation needs after you've consumed. This will allow you to relax, enjoy the party, and mingle. After all, you're there to meet other people who like pot. Feel confident introducing yourself and remember you have some easy low-hanging fruit to reach for when it comes to conversation starters: "What's your cannabis preference?" "What strains are you drawn to?" "What's your go-to method?"

I Doobie Do: Weed & Weddings

For those who consume cannabis or live in legalized states, weed at weddings is a very common occurrence. While the presence of cannabis can range from a designated consumption area to having a fully setup bud bar complete with budtenders and cannabis parting gifts, it's safe to say weed is a new trending topic for wedding planning.

DECIDING HOW FAR TO TAKE IT

How far to go with offering cannabis consumption at your wedding is really up to you and your budget. The big things to consider are your wishes and your guests' comfort. Beyond that, you could have a fully cannabis-incorporated wedding: infused dinner and cocktails, a toke toast, welcome gifts and thank-you gifts (both to be consumed in-state), education station, and a full-on bud bar (costs are covered by the host). You really can go all out (easier when there are no underage guests). But for most 420-friendly weddings, you'll see as a guest or decide as a host to provide a designated cannabis area.

GETTING THE WORD OUT

It's important to prepare guests for what they are walking into. Many couples state that their family and friends either know that they are cannabis friendly or that they wouldn't be surprised if cannabis were to be served at a private event in a legalized state. Acceptance and understanding aside, it's good to give guests who are less familiar with legalized cannabis culture a heads-up. Adding information about the reception, ceremony, and local flavor along with other pertinent details to a page on your wedding website or including it in an insert along with the invitation would be perfectly appropriate. Invite guests to ask you questions if they are curious and reassure those who are worried that they aren't about to be hotboxed or clambaked (when you fill a small unventilated space full of smoke) into consuming. (See Contact

Highs? on page 62 to see why this requires a lot—A LOT—of smoke to actually create an effect other than inhaling a lot of carcinogenic secondhand smoke.)

Things to mention: information about to what extent cannabis will be part of the event and basic state and local laws are a good place to start. You can also provide dispensary and cannactivity information.

TRANSPORTATION

Similar to weddings where alcohol is served, it's important to think about safety and transportation. While you may leave it up to your guests' discretion, a good host provides some services, as much as their budget allows, and if you're creating a very 420-friendly atmosphere at your wedding, you should consider how to get your guests home safely.

SETUP & MONITORING

Your setup can range from a sign that says, "Please consume cannabis over there" to a properly sectioned-off area or room at the reception with a person on hand to make sure that no one underage consumes. The presence of children makes most canna-wedding couples decide to section off a part of the reception for cannabis consumption. By having a defined boundary and by assigning someone to keep watch over the area you can ensure that the cannabis section of the party stays adult only.

Be sure to label everything you serve your guests and make sure that any gifts they are sent "home" with are properly sealed and labeled with strain, potency, and effect.

AS A GUEST . . .

- Feel comfortable participating in anything the hosts are offering (or not).

- Be mindful of consumption areas and stay in them when consuming.

- Remember to keep the focus on celebrating the couple (not just the free weed).

- If the couple consumes, a cannabis-related product or piece of equipment or a cannabis experience would make a great wedding gift.

HIGHER ETIQUETTE TIP

Offer guests information on local dispensaries and events that might be fun while they are in town. Provide newbies who might use your wedding as a weedcation with some helpful tips and safety warnings. Preparing a card that highlights the differences between edibles and inhalation or giving a guide to the number of milligrams or grams to consume can help your guests have a fun and safe experience during your wedding.

Weedcations

Taking a vacation purely to go explore and engage more with ganja is a dream come legally true for cannabis enthusiasts. When going on a weedcation to experience all the legalized world of cannabis has to offer, there are some fun things to explore and there is some higher etiquette to keep in mind.

SEVEN TIPS FOR A SUCCESSFUL WEEDCATION

Here are seven things to consider when on a weedcation that will help make it a truly fun, memorable, and safe experience:

1. **Prepare.** Depending on the state you are traveling to, you'll want to look up their cannabis consumption laws. Going on a weedcation in a state where they don't have a retail and regulation system set up is no good, unless you have a local friend who grows their own. Check that your destination legally offers the kind of experience you're looking for. Look for hotels and vacation rentals that are 420-friendly so that you can feel confident experimenting in the place you're staying.

2. **Be aware of elevation and climate impact.** Remember that if you are traveling to a new state and consuming cannabis, pay attention to the elevation and climate differences. Getting high at 8,000 feet as opposed to sea level or in a hot climate as opposed to a mild one means cannabis may have more of an impact.

3. **Remember the interstate rules.** You can't bring product or used equipment across state lines, and talking about doing so or even asking about it at a dispensary might result in your having to leave the premises.

4. **Be sure to have proper ID.** To make any purchases or to go on any tours, you'll need a valid photo ID.

5. **Be respectful.** While enjoying legalized consumption is incredibly cool and fun, it's also a respected part of people's everyday lives. Going into a dispensary and mocking or making fun of cannabis culture is not polite, and those around you will not appreciate your making jokes about cannabis being a drug.

6. **Keep it level.** While a weedcation should be about exploring the world of cannabis, don't forget to pace yourself and check in with your group about how people are managing their cannabis consumption. It doesn't have to be ganja galore.

7. **Drink water.** Staying hydrated will help you have a blast throughout your entire weedcation experience.

CANNA-BUS TOURS

Cannabis bus tours are a fun way to enjoy cannabis, visit some cannabis grows or dispensaries, learn, and, of course, sample lots of product. These buses usually have a tour guide, a few groups of tourists on the tour, and make a number of stops. Three things to consider:

1. **Pay attention to your guide.** Once on the bus, it's very easy to become engaged with your friends; however, you should listen to the information your tour guide is providing and be respectful of her instructions. You should ask questions and engage with her—guides usually welcome those exchanges and find it preferable to having groups who only chat among themselves.

2. **Mix it up.** While tour bus riders will often sit in the same seat between stops, as long as someone's personal belongings aren't

occupying a seat, it's fine to switch seats and get to know others on the tour. If someone doesn't seem particularly chatty, that's okay, too; just move back to your own group or strike up a conversation with another person.

3. **Tip your guide.** As with most tours, it's considerate to tip your guide before you leave. Depending on the cost of the tour, you might tip anywhere from 10 to 20 percent of the cost of your group or individual ticket price or $5 to $20, depending on the type of tour and the guide. Some guides may not accept gratuities. It's always nice to start a tipping interaction with, "Thank you so much for today. May I ask if you accept tips?"

GROW TOUR ETIQUETTE

Visiting a grow operation comes with its own etiquette. Because plants are delicate and prone to cross-contamination, it's important to pay attention and respect the rules the growers set forth for their facility or farm. That said, it can be a fascinating and educational experience to visit a grower and can really deepen your appreciation for cannabis production.

The number one rule when visiting a grow operation is not to touch *anything*, especially the plants, since the oils on your skin and pressure from your fingers could damage them. Similarly, always cough or sneeze into your elbow. It's respectful to both the plants and to the people on the tour.

Cross-contamination is the biggest concern for a grower, so be aware that you may be asked where you've traveled to that day or asked to change before starting a tour. Some facilities may even issue scrubs to all visitors in order to eliminate the concern for cross-contamination.

Questions are welcome at appropriate moments on the tour—the people who work at these operation are often very knowledgeable about and proud of their plants and enjoy sharing what they know.

RESOURCES

Here are some resources you may find interesting and useful as you continue to explore cannabis.

Books

Cannabis Cocktails, Mocktails & Tonics: The Art of Spirited Drinks & Buzz-Worthy Libations. Warren Bobrow, Fair Winds Press, 2016.

The Cannabis Manifesto: A New Paradigm for Wellness. Steve DeAngelo, North Atlantic Books, 2015.

Grow Your Own: Understanding, Cultivating, and Enjoying Cannabis. Nichole Graf, Micah Sherman, David Stein, and Liz Crain, Tin House Books, 2017.

Articles

"How to Customize Your Cannabis High with Temperature." Bailey Rahn, medithrive.com/customize-your-cannabis-high.

"Vaping vs. Dabbing: Why You Should Care About Heat." Anna Wilcox, www.leafly.com/news/cannabis-101/vaping-versus-dabbing-why-you-should-care-about-heat.

"What's in a strain name? Is Highlighting Cannabis Outcome Detrimental To Growers And Production Techniques?" Zoe Wilder, bigbudsmag.com/indica-sativa-why-focusing-on-strain-is-passe.

Websites

Leafly, Leafly.com

Goldleaf, Shopgoldleaf.com

Phylos Bioscience, Phylos.bio

Sativa Science Club, Sativascienceclub.com

Trichome Institute, Trichomeinstitute.com

ACKNOWLEDGMENTS

This book would not have been possible without the many people who contributed their time and knowledge to it. I was blown away by the generosity of spirit and genuine support that I received when working on this project. It is with deep gratitude and appreciation that I acknowledge the following people for their contributions, not only in their specific area of expertise but also for their enthusiasm and encouragement.

My cousin and copresident at the Emily Post Institute, **Daniel Post Senning**, who long ago talked with me about this idea being something that would one day happen. Dan, that day is here and I want to thank you for all you've done to help make it a reality.

My parents, **Tricia** and **Peter Post**, who were absolute in their belief that this book was needed. You read every draft and offered thoughtful (and humorous) feedback. Thank you for being supportive and encouraging from day one . . . my entire life.

My aunt **Peggy Post**, who without a doubt has been one of the book's biggest supporters and advocates. And my sister, **Anna Post**, for your keen eye and opinions on color and design.

My agents, **Katherine Cowles** of Cowles Literary Agency, who is far more than an agent and brand manager, and **Brandi Bowles** of United Talent Agency, who initiated this project. Thank you both for your support and your confidence.

Kaitlin Ketchum, my editor at Ten Speed Press, holy awesome editing, batgirl—working with you has been inspiring and incredibly fun! I thank you for your attention to detail, your understanding and support, and especially your good humor.

The Ten Speed Press Team: designer **Lizzie Allen**, publicist **David Hawk**, marketing manager **Daniel Wikey**, and production manager **Jane Chinn**. Thanks also to copy editor **Dolores York** and proofreader **Ellen Cavalli**.

Sam Kalda, the book's illustrator, thank you for taking my odd sample illustrations and descriptions and turning them into something clever, fun, and classy.

The January 2018 staff at **Magnolia Road Cannabis Company**, for hosting me for a week at the dispensary and giving detailed interviews, especially **Christian Preston** (and his amazing mother, **Deetra Preston**), **Jackson Howard**, and **John Szalwinski** as well as **Will White, Clark Tucher, Erica Martinez, Jason Sweger, Ian Becker, Luke Weathersby, Wenze Bo, Justin Howard, Amanda Barnes**, and **Liz Boutin**.

Neal "Fro" Evans and **Eric Wolf,** for hosting me and letting me throw a research party all about weed at your house. I'd also like to thank your many friends who attended, especially **Matthew Volkes** who smoked me up out of a sweet potato.

Casey, Satya, and **Tanya** (and **Mergatroid**), my Colorado Post family members who hosted me during research. Thank you for giving me your time, your friends' time, your knowledge, your Subaru WRX Turbo, and some fun target practice.

Dan Martin, founder/owner of Magnolia Road Cannabis Company in Colorado, you have been my guide from the moment I said "yes" to this project. Thank you for being so accessible, accommodating, and generous for the past year. To Dan's family: **Jennifer, Lyric, Haddie,** and **Lucie,** thank you for your generosity, hospitality, and especially your insight. Our family meals together and the discussions about living and growing up in a legalized state were so impactful.

Dawn Zig Zag Montefusco, my longtime friend and mentor, thank you for always saying yes and connecting so many amazing people. **Joe Bazegi** of Manna Cannabis and **Christian Fooks** of Cut & Dry Systems, for your chivalrous natures and unwavering patience (and humor) while escorting me on tours of Portland's pot scene.

Tito Anders, my superhero, for organizing and hosting a focus group of fabulous people for my Portland research. Thank you to those who participated: **Tad, Leslie, Geoffrey, Selena, Dawn, Joe, Mark, Tara,** and **Elliot**.

My friend **Jon,** for encouraging me and providing me with my very first legalized recreational dispensary experience.

To the many people I interviewed, on the phone and in person, who tolerated my conversational tangents, thank you for giving your perspective, your knowledge, and your time to help me make this book happen:

Zoe Wilder, writer, publicist, and communications professional, my gratitude goes beyond words for the connections you made and the help you gave me.

Emma Chasen, cannabis educator and consultant, thank you for taking the time to truly teach me about the science of cannabis and forever change how I look at it.

Ky Dumont of Kyla Emily Skincare and my dear friend, thank you for your invaluable help with the proposal for this book and your unwavering support for the politeness of pot. My friend **Geordie Schuurman** of Left Field; **Ry Prichard**, cannabis expert and consultant specializing in strain and concentrate knowledge and cohost of *Bong Appétit*; **Will Hyde**, cannabis expert and cohost of Leafly.com's podcast *What Are You Smoking?*; **Elise McRoberts**, cannabist activist, influencer, and delivery chief for California Wellness; **Anja Charbonneau**, founder of *Broccoli* magazine; **Stephanie Madewell**, my editor at *Broccoli*; **Charles McElroy** at Goldleaf; **Philip Wolf** of Cultivating Spirits—you would have made Emily Post proud! **Aviv Hadir** of Oregrown (possibly one of the book's most enthusiastic supporters!); **Jen Bernstein**, former managing editor at *High Times* magazine, your activism has made a difference to millions. **Bridgit Conry** and **Shayne Lynn** of Champlain Valley Dispensary + Southern Vermont Wellness; **Stacey Mulvey** of Marijuasana; **Doreen Sullivan** of My Bud Vase; **Dr. Ryan Vandrey** at John's Hopkins University; **Katie Stem** and **Kate Black** of Peak Extracts; **Zane Witzel** of Cannador; **Brad Blommer** and **Perry Salzhauer** of Green Light Law Group; **Dakota Sheets**, founder of Resolution; **Stephen Gold** and **Andy Yashar** of Fore Twenty Sports; **Jessie Gill** of Marijuana Mommy; **Bill Stewart** of The Doctor's House Bud 'N' Breakfast in Oregon; **Tae Darnell** of *Sensi Magazine* and Hoban Law Group; **Jason Zaworski**; **Jenna Lynn Roberts**, my AirBnB host in Portland and a wonderful fellow writer; **Nichole Graff** of Raven Grass and co-author of *Grow Your Own*; **Liz Crain**, coauthor of *Grow Your Own*;

Zoe Sigman, codirector of education at Farma; **Danny Sloat** and **Kristin Murr** of AlpinStash; **Warren Bobrow**, author of *Cannabis Cocktails, Mocktails & Tonics*; **Lauren Miele** of KushKards; **Jessica Cole** of White Rabbit High Teas; **Jason Schnepple** of Advanced Extracts; my longtime friends and canna-sisters, **Jane Jarecki Lanza** and **Peach. Kelly Williams Brown**, my dear friend, thank you for emergency author calls; and a very special thank-you goes to **Ellen Hoos** at Silverpeak Apothecary, whose dream that, one day, cannabis will be served at cafes will surely come true.

Kayla and **Trenton**, thank you for tolerating living with me while I researched and wrote this book.

Special thanks to my dear friend **JJJJJJJJJJJPPPPPPPPPPP**!

To my larger **Post family** and **Susan Iverson** at the Emily Post Institute, thank you for your support and encouragement throughout this process. **Nadia Hucko**, who interned at Emily Post and worked almost exclusively on this book during your time with us, helping with research, images, and perspective, deserves a very large thank-you. As does **Caroline Noll**, who interned and assisted with the proposal process.

To my very large **Flynn family**, thank you for being excited and for continuing to support my interest in this topic. "When you're on the farm, you're on the farm!"

Thank you to those who are unnamed but nonetheless important in the making of this book. Every plane, train, bar stool, and dispensary conversation about cannabis etiquette helped to round out the perspective, and I am looking forward to having so many more conversations and broadening these pages as cannabis becomes fully legalized in America.

ABOUT THE AUTHOR

Lizzie Post is the great-great-granddaughter of American etiquette expert Emily Post. The copresident of the Emily Post Institute and author and co-author of several books on etiquette, Lizzie delights in being the cohost of the Institute's *Awesome Etiquette* podcast and is very happy to live in her home state of Vermont, which legalized cannabis through legislation in 2018.

INDEX

Copyright © 2019 by Lizzie Post
Illustrations copyright © 2019 by Sam Kalda

Published in the United States by Ten Speed Press, an imprint
of the Crown Publishing Group, a division of Penguin Random
House LLC, New York.
www.crownpublishing.com
www.tenspeed.com

Ten Speed Press and the Ten Speed Press colophon are
registered trademarks of Penguin Random House LLC.

Library of Congress Cataloging-in-Publication Data is on file
with the publisher.

Hardcover ISBN: 978-0-399-58239-4
eBook ISBN: 978-0-399-58240-0

Printed in China

Design by Lizzie Allen

10 9 8 7 6 5 4 3 2 1

First Edition

Emily Post

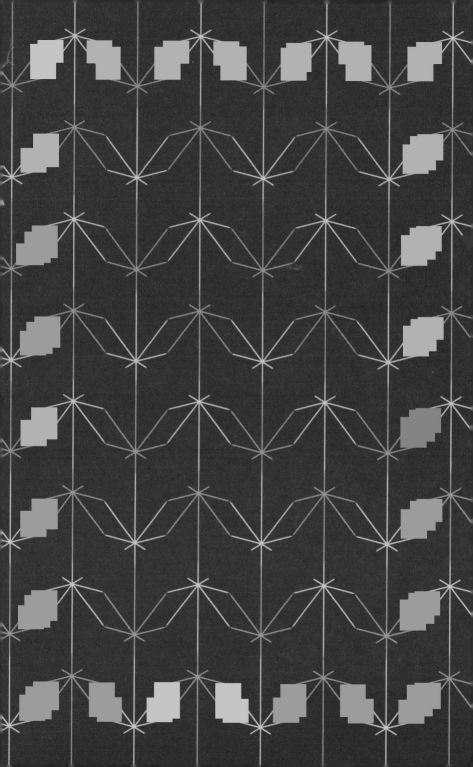